TODAY'sKITCHEN
COOKBOOK

Meredith® Books
Des Moines, Iowa

very special thanks to: Katie Couric, Matt Lauer, Al Roker, Ann Curry, Bob Wright, Jeff Zucker, Neal Shapiro, Frederick Huntsberry, Jerry Petry, Phil Griffin, Jim Bell, David McCormick, Bill Wheatley, Lauren Kapp, Deborah Warren

This book would not be possible without the support of the talented chefs and featured celebrity chefs who appear in the book and who enabled NBC to donate proceeds from the sale of the book to the T.J. Martell Foundation.

PRODUCT DEVELOPMENT AND DIRECTION: Frank Radice, Kim Niemi
PROJECT COORDINATORS: Neysa Gordon, Jenna Tyre

This was a truly collaborative effort, and we thank the many people who gave their time and energy to this project: Jacqueline Agnolet, Betsy Alexander, Tammy Blake, Anka Brazzell, Jenness Brewer, April Brock, Vicky Brown, Tim Bruno, Alison Buckley, Caryn Burtt, Brendan Carretta, Shannon Chaiken-Huyter, Cindy Chang, Bari Cohen, Eileen Connors, Doe Coover, Danielle Costa, Linda Cunningham, Arlyn Davich, Anne Dolamore, Laurie Dolphin, Janis Donnaud, Suzanna de Jong, Georgette Farkas, Kate Fox, Grayce Galioto, Anthony Gardner, Gina Gargano, Alfred Geller, Beth Goss, Emily Gould, Kristen Gross, Rosie Gurock, Bill Hartnett, Rebecca Heisman, Shelli Hill, Yukari Hirata, Marisa Huff, Meghan Hurley, Devin Johnson, Leslie Jonath, Helen Jorda, Frances Kennedy, Pam Krauss, Robin Lawson, Bill LeBlond, Pam Lewy, David Lipsius, Ron Longe, Vince Manze, Chloe Mata, Mark McBride, Sandi Mendelson, Jan Miller, John Miller, Lauren Mitchell, George Nunes, Chris Pavone, Otto Petersen, Zinta Poilovs, Liz Ravage, Caroline Riordan, Talia Rosen, Linda Ross, Marissa Sanchez, Sophie Schrager, Will Schwalbe, Ann Sherwood, Traecy Smith, Caroline Somers, Lisa A. Sommer, Kelly Sparwasser, Cressida Suttles, Tom Touchet, Sonja Toulouse, Kevin Toyama, Kate Tyler, Kimberly Yorio

Thanks to our friends with T.J. Martell: Tony Martell, Debbie Martell, Lou Mann, Elayne Periharos, Peter Quinn

Tony Martell Thanks: Everyone at the *TODAY* Show and NBC for all their hard work on this project. A toast to all the wonderful chefs and celebrities for their mouthwatering recipes. A special thank you to my daughter Debbie Martell, T.J.'s sister, for her wonderful recipe. I am so proud of her contribution to our vital cause. I am extremely grateful to Peter Quinn and Elayne Periharos at the Foundation for working tirelessly to make this happen. My profound thanks to everyone who purchased this book.

SENIOR EDITOR: Stephanie Karpinske
CO-EDITOR/CONTRIBUTING PHOTOGRAPHER: Laurie Dolphin
SENIOR ASSOCIATE DESIGN DIRECTOR: Mick Schnepf
COVER PHOTOGRAPH: George Lange **FOOD PHOTOGRAPHS:** Scott Little, Blaine Moats
CONTRIBUTING DESIGNER: Chad Johnston
MARKETING DIRECTOR: Amy Nichols **MARKETING PRODUCT MANAGER:** Gina Rickert
VISIT US AT: www.meredithbooks.com

> contents

>foreword

Over the years **TODAY's** KITCHEN has been one of the highlights of our mornings. It's been fun and exciting to have such an array of talented chefs grace our studio and fill our stomachs. We love to cook (with varying degrees of success), but when it comes to eating—that's something everyone enjoys! By nine o'clock it feels like lunchtime and we're ravenous. The wonderful dishes that are whipped up on an almost daily basis give a whole new meaning to the term "breakfast of champions"!

Food is such an integral part of our lives; not only does it nourish the body, but it nourishes the soul. Whether it's a cozy Sunday night supper, a lavish holiday feast, a healthy breakfast, or a summer picnic for two—we've done it all on *Today* and hope we've helped many families create new memories and traditions. In our increasingly hectic and stressed-out lives, sharing a meal can be one of life's greatest pleasures. Good food often leads to good conversations; good conversations often lead to renewed relationships. Even the process of preparing a meal—whether it's peeling potatoes or setting a table—can be part of time-honored rituals and traditions that keep us grounded, sane, and connected.

We hope the recipes in this book will help you stop and smell if not the roses, perhaps the fragrant Chile-Rubbed Brisket (p. 111) or Country Plum Cake (p. 151). And while you are eating well, you are doing good! A portion of the proceeds from the sales of this book will be donated to the T.J. Martell Foundation, which raises funds to support innovative and ongoing research into treatments and cures for leukemia, cancer, and AIDS. We decided this was a wonderful organization worthy of our support and yours.

Thanks to the generosity of the many talented chefs who've appeared on our show, many of the delicious dishes you've seen on *Today* can move from our kitchen to yours. So dive in, roll up your sleeves, and most of all ... enjoy!

Katie Couric, *Matt Lauer,* *Al Roker,* *Ann Curry*

You hold in your hands much more than an amazing cookbook! Not only does it offer extraordinary and diverse recipes for you and your family, but when you purchase this book, a portion of the proceeds go directly to the **T.J. Martell Foundation** for leukemia, cancer, and AIDS Research.

The foundation was created in 1975 in honor of my son T.J. who, at too young of an age, lost his long battle with leukemia. Before his death he asked me to promise to raise $1 million to help find a cure. Of course I said yes, not having a clue how I was going to achieve this. With the help of my friends and colleagues in the music and entertainment industry, the foundation has blossomed into one of the most prominent charities in its field. As we celebrate our 30th anniversary, we are funding eight leading research facilities nationwide and have raised more than $200 million for vital research to find cures and treatments for these devastating diseases.

We have made a difference. Today the type of leukemia T.J. had is not only treatable but in most cases is curable. We are now looking toward a breakthrough in the treatment of colon cancer. That is the goal we hope to achieve with the funds raised from this book.

Ironically, my daughter, Debbie, went on to graduate from The Culinary Institute of America and received a degree in nutrition at Arizona State University. She is a Performance Chef at Athletes' Performance in Tempe, Arizona. Debbie has combined her vast culinary and dietetic expertise to create menus that are healthy and nutritious without compromising the pleasure of great taste. She works with elite professional and amateur athletes. I am truly proud that she has contributed to this outstanding cookbook that includes famous culinary names as well as celebrities.

On behalf of everyone stricken with cancer, I would like to thank the *Today* show for making the T.J. Martell Foundation the beneficiary of the sales of this book. With your help we will find a cure.

I hope you enjoy this treasury of delicious recipes. I know I will. This is truly a taste of *Today*. Bon Appetit!

Sincerely, *Tony Martell, Chairman*

Barley "Risotto"
with spinach, tomatoes & chickpeas

Debbie Martell

1/3 yellow onion, chopped
1 teaspoon extra-virgin olive oil
1 cup pearled barley
3 cups fat-free chicken broth
  (may need a little more)
2 roma tomatoes, coarsely chopped
1 frozen 10-ounce package chopped spinach, thawed
1 can chickpeas (drained)
1 tablespoon Parmesan cheese, grated
  Salt and pepper to taste

IN a medium pot, sauté onion with olive oil until wilted. Add barley and stir to coat.

ADD stock. Bring to a boil, reduce heat to simmer and cover.

SIMMER for approximately 45 minutes, stirring frequently to make sure broth has not evaporated.

ADD spinach, tomatoes and chickpeas. Mix together. Simmer for 5 more minutes.

BARLEY should have a "bite" to it, and there should be a small amount of broth left.

KEEP on the heat longer with more broth if barley is not cooked enough for your taste.

TAKE off heat; stir in Parmesan. Season with salt and pepper.
serves 4 (side-dish servings)

" As someone who is very conscious about eating right and feeling healthy and energized, Debbie allowed me to have great healthy meals that were still good portion sizes and tasted awesome. She could take the foods I liked and was allowed to eat and created something really delicious. The pizza she made was my favorite. " —*Jennifer Capriati*

Vanessa Williams > Potato Pancakes

Cold water
4 large potatoes (peeled and rinsed)
1 onion
2 eggs
$\frac{1}{3}$ cup flour
2 teaspoons salt
$\frac{1}{8}$ teaspoon pepper
$\frac{1}{3}$ cup salad oil
Apple sauce or sour cream for dipping (optional)

SHRED potatoes and onion into a large bowl half filled with cold water. Pour into a colander lined with cheesecloth. Wrap the towel and squeeze the excess water out. Put potato mixture back into bowl and add eggs, flour, salt and pepper.

MAKE 12-inch skillet medium hot with salad oil and drop mixture in to make pancakes. Flatten with spatula and turn when golden brown. Remove and drain on towel-lined cookie sheet. **serves about 12**

Sfihas (Meat Tarts)
and fried cauliflower

< **C**eline **D**ion

Dough
1 can Pillsbury® Refrigerated Crescent Dinner Rolls

Stuffing
1 pound ground veal
1 medium onion, finely chopped
¼ cup plain yogurt
2 tablespoons pine nuts, roasted
1 egg
Salt to taste
Arabian Pepper to taste (finely milled white and black pepper, cardamom, nutmeg, 4-spices, cloves and cinnamon) (available in specialty food shops)

HEAT oven to 425°F.

REMOVE dough from can and divide each triangle strip in half. Shape dough into 3-inch diameter tarts and flatten edges, leaving the center thicker. Mix all stuffing ingredients with hands. Spread mixture on dough circles to within ¼-inch of edge.

PLACE sfihas on greased cookie sheet and bake 7 to 10 minutes on lower rack. Shift cookie sheet to upper rack and bake 5 minutes.

SERVE with Fried Cauliflower.
makes 16

Fried Cauliflower
2 large heads cauliflower, cut in florets
Vegetable oil, for frying
Salt and Arabian Pepper

HEAT oil to 375°F. Fry cauliflower until golden brown. Pat dry on a paper towel. Season with salt and Arabian Pepper.

Sharon Osbourne > Shepard's Pie
with rosemary mash

2 pounds minced lamb
1/2 ounce butter
2 medium onions, finely diced
2 cloves garlic, finely chopped
4 carrots, chopped
1 teaspoon thyme leaves
1/2 tablespoon plain flour
1 tablespoon tomato puree
1 14 1/2-ounce can chopped
  tomatoes
3/4 pint chicken/lamb stock
1 tablespoon Worcestershire
  sauce
3 pounds potatoes (peeled,
  chopped into large chunks)
1/4 pint milk
1/4 pint cream
1 ounce butter
2 sprigs rosemary

HEAT large pan with a little oil. Fry minced lamb until golden; drain and remove from pan.

HEAT butter. When hot, add onions, garlic, carrots and thyme leaves and cook for about 2 minutes. Then add back minced lamb with flour and tomato puree. Cook for a further 2 minutes. Then add chopped tomatoes, stock and Worcestershire sauce. Cook on very low heat for 30 to 40 minutes.

MEANWHILE boil potatoes in salted water. When cooked, drain. Mash potatoes with milk, cream and butter; add rosemary. Season with salt and pepper.

PLACE cooked minced lamb into an oven-proof serving dish. Place layer of cooked mash on top. Grill until golden brown. **serves 2 to 4**

Joe Perry's Hard Rock Cafe Rock Your World Quesadilla

Joe **P**erry

5 ounces chicken breast
1/2 teaspoon salad oil
1/4 teaspoon kosher salt
Pinch ground black pepper
1 cup Monterey Jack cheese, shredded
1 10-inch flour tortilla, warmed
1/4 cup Grilled Pineapple
3 tablespoons Tango Sauce
2 tablespoons Spicy Fruit Salsa
2 tablespoons sour cream (optional)
2 tablespoons guacamole (optional)

OIL and season each side of chicken breast with salad oil, salt and pepper. Grill chicken on hot oiled grill on both sides. Cook to 165°F.

SPREAD cheese evenly on the tortilla. Toss together chicken slices, Grilled Pineapple and 2 tablespoons of Tango Sauce. Pour onto half of tortilla. Place under broiler. Broil until cheese boils.

REMOVE quesadilla from the heat and fold in half. Cut quesadilla into 3 to 4 equal triangles, then place on platter.

PLACE 2 tablespoons of Spicy Fruit Salsa, sour cream and guacamole on platter. Drizzle remaining Tango Sauce on platter. **makes 1**

Grilled Pineapple

CUT one **pineapple,** approximately 1/2 inch from the bottom and the base of the green leaves. Remove skin. Slice pineapple into 1/2-inch slices and toss with 2 tablespoons **salad oil** and 1 tablespoon **chili powder**. Place pineapple slices on hot grill. Turn the slices to form crisscross grill marks on both sides. Cut out and discard the core from each slice. Cut fruit into small cubes.

Tango Sauce

STIR together 1 cup of your favorite **BBQ sauce** and 1/4 cup **Joe Perry's Mango Peach Tango Sauce.**

Spicy Fruit Salsa

DRAIN one 15 1/4-ounce can **Dole Tropical Fruit Salad.** Place the fruit into a food processor and pulse until chopped to randomly smaller pieces (approximately 1/4 to 1/2 inch). NOTE: DO NOT PUREE THE FRUIT. Toss fruit with 2 tablespoons **Joe Perry's Rock Your World Mango Peach Tango Hot Sauce.**

one

Simple, Healthy & Quick

Q&A

Katie Couric >

Q. Where did you learn to cook?

A. I learned to cook from my mom growing up.

Q. What is your first memory of cooking?

A. My brother and I made omelettes. I was an omelette freak for years! I also remember making dinner for my parents. Fried chicken was the main course and chocolate pudding was dessert. I spent many Saturdays baking chocolate chip cookies with my friends—unfortunately, I ate most of the dough!

Q. Do you follow recipes or do you just like to experiment?

A. I follow recipes and I experiment—often the latter ends in disaster! I like to experiment with salads—mixing in nuts, dried fruit, fresh fruit, and exotic vegetables like jicama.

Q. What is your favorite recipe and where did you get it?

A. I'm not a great cook, but I like making Lemon Chicken. I saw Gary Collins prepare it on a show, *Hour Magazine,* many years ago. Sometimes I make it with Dijon instead of lemons. It's a very versatile dish!

Q. What meals do you make for your kids that they love?

A. Breakfasts! (Which Carrie used to call breafkiss!) I love making eggs and bacon or pancakes, and sometimes this not particularly healthy dish we call "little biscuits"! I cut up biscuits, fry them in butter, and pour syrup, cinnamon, and sugar on top. I only make it for special occasions for obvious reasons!

Q. What is your favorite gourmet meal to eat or prepare?

A. Fresh Maine lobster with lots of butter and lemon and with corn and tomatoes.

Q. What do you make when you are entertaining guests? Why?

A. I rarely entertain, but I like ham and biscuits, grits, southern foods ... my mom makes a killer homemade mustard.

Q. What are your favorite spices for cooking?

A. I LOVE fresh cilantro! Especially in homemade salsa! I also like ginger, curry, and lemongrass. And I love dishes made with coconut.

Q. Has your style of cooking changed over the years? If so, what influenced the change?

A. No—I like oldies but goodies when it comes to recipes. I try to eat and cook healthy. Lately I have been trying to get more soy in my diet.

Q. Since you have traveled across the globe, what is your favorite regional cuisine?

A. I love the spices used in Thai food. My first date with my husband was at a Thai restaurant in Washington, D.C.

Q. What is your favorite comfort food?

A. Bacon! Turkey chili isn't bad either.

Q. What is the food that you should not eat but do?

A. Bacon!!!

Q. What do you eat for breakfast before the show?

A. During the show I usually have Shredded Wheat, Grape-Nuts, or a hard-boiled egg or toast with peanut butter for a little protein boost.

Katie's Lemon Chicken <Katie Couric

4 boneless, skinless chicken
   breasts
   Flour for dredging
2 tablespoons butter
2 tablespoons olive oil
3 tablespoons flour
   Juice of 2 lemons
3 cups chicken broth
   Salt and ground white
   pepper to taste
   Hot cooked basmati rice
   Chopped fresh parsley
   Lemon slices

POUND chicken breasts with meat pounder to a uniform thickness. Dredge lightly in flour, shaking off excess.

IN a large sauté pan over medium-high heat, melt the butter and oil until it sizzles. Add the chicken breasts and sauté, turning once or twice, until cooked through and juices run clear. Remove chicken and set aside.

WHISK in flour and cook for 1 minute until the mixture boils.

ADD lemon juice to the chicken broth and whisk into sauté pan. Reduce heat to a simmer.

RETURN chicken to pan to heat through, thickening sauce to desired consistency. Season to taste with salt and ground white pepper.

SERVE the chicken on a bed of basmati rice and spoon the sauce over the chicken. Garnish with chopped parsley and lemon slices.
serves 4

Roasted Pepper Salad
with basil and mint

<Kathleen Daelemans

2 pounds red peppers (4 to
   5 large peppers)
2 tablespoons olive oil
1 tablespoon balsamic vinegar
2 tablespoons fresh lemon juice
1/4 cup loosely packed roughly
   chopped fresh basil and mint
   Coarse grained salt and
   cracked black pepper

PREHEAT broiler to high. Core and cut peppers into quarters; remove seeds and membranes.

PLACE on a nonstick baking sheet under broiler until skins blacken slightly. Place hot peppers in a plastic bag, seal and let stand 15 minutes. When cool enough to handle, remove skin from peppers. Place peeled peppers in serving dish.

IN a small bowl, whisk together oil, vinegar, lemon juice, herbs, salt and pepper. Taste; adjust seasonings. Pour over peppers.

SERVE immediately or let stand at room temperature up to four hours. **serves 4**

Chef Tip: Grab a baguette, slice it in half lengthwise, load it up with a layer of this salad, some arugula or any salad greens, and thinly sliced skim milk mozzarella cheese, leftover cooked chicken breast, or steak.

Sara **C**orpening **W**hiteford
& **M**ary **C**orpening **B**arber **>** Summer Tomato Stack

4 ounces fresh mozzarella cheese
½ cup balsamic vinegar
  Kosher salt and freshly
  ground pepper
2 small ripe summer tomatoes
  (about 4 ounces each),
  stems attached
1 teaspoon extra-virgin olive oil
8 large fresh basil leaves

SLICE the mozzarella into four
½-inch-thick slices and set them
on a paper towel-lined plate to
drain. Blot the cheese with paper
towels to remove excess moisture.

HEAT the balsamic vinegar with a
pinch of kosher salt and a pinch of
pepper in a small heavy-bottomed
saucepan over medium-high heat.

COOK at a moderate boil until
reduced to 1 tablespoon, about
7 minutes. (Watch carefully to avoid
overreducing. The reduction is
complete when the vinegar coats
the bottom of the pan yet still flows
freely. It will thicken as it cools.)
Immediately transfer the vinegar
to a small bowl.

CUT a very thin slice from the
bottom of each tomato to create
a flat surface. Discard. Cut each
tomato into 3 slices. Place the
bottom slice of each tomato on a
serving plate. Drizzle each slice
with ¼ teaspoon of the olive oil.
Season generously with kosher

salt and pepper to taste. Top each
slice with 2 basil leaves and a slice
of mozzarella. Season the cheese
generously with kosher salt and
pepper to taste. Create another
layer following the same process,
using the middle slice of each
tomato. Top the stacks with the
remaining slices, stem sides up.
Just before serving, decoratively
drizzle the balsamic syrup around
the tomato stack. **serves 2**

Chef Tip: If you reduce the balsamic
vinegar too much so that it is too thick
to pour when cooled, simply stir in a
few more drops of vinegar. Use the
ripest, most picture-perfect tomatoes
you can find and purchase only fresh,
preferably water-packed mozzarella.

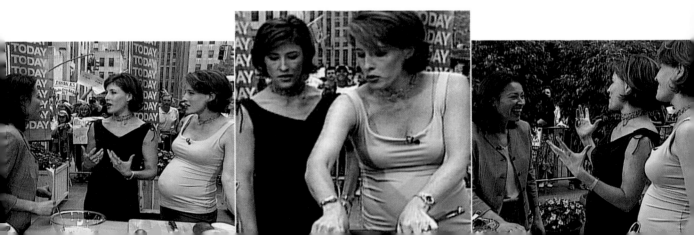

Baked Goat Cheese <Alice Waters
with garden lettuces

½ pound fresh goat cheese
(one 2×5-inch log)
½ cup extra-virgin olive oil
3 to 4 sprigs fresh thyme,
chopped
1 small sprig rosemary, chopped
½ sour baguette
1 tablespoon red wine vinegar
1 teaspoon sherry vinegar
Salt and pepper
½ cup extra-virgin olive oil
½ pound local, organic garden
lettuces, washed and dried

CAREFULLY slice the goat cheese into 8 disks about 1 inch thick. Pour the olive oil over the disks and sprinkle with the chopped herbs. Cover and store in a cool place for several hours.

PREHEAT the oven to 300°F. Cut the baguette in half lengthwise and dry out in the oven for 20 minutes or so, until dry and lightly colored. Grate into fine crumbs on a box grater or in a food processor. The crumbs can be made in advance and stored until needed.

PREHEAT the oven to 400°F. (A toaster oven works well.) Remove the cheese disks from the marinade and roll them in the bread crumbs, coating them thoroughly.

PLACE the cheese on a small baking sheet and bake for about 6 minutes, until the cheese is warm.

MEASURE the vinegars into a small bowl and add a big pinch of salt. Whisk in the oil and a little freshly ground pepper. Taste for seasoning and adjust.

TOSS the lettuces lightly with the vinaigrette and arrange on salad plates.

WITH a metal spatula, carefully place 2 disks of the baked cheese on each plate and serve. **serves 4**

Chef Tip: Be sure to select a goat cheese that is firm enough to be sliced.

Orzo Salad ◄ Ellen Carroll
with corn, tomatoes, and basil

Dressing
- 2 tablespoons fresh lemon juice
- 1 tablespoon olive oil
- 1 teaspoon red wine vinegar
- ½ teaspoon salt
- ¼ teaspoon black pepper
- 3 cloves garlic, crushed

Salad
- 1 cup uncooked orzo (rice-shape pasta)
- 2 cups fresh yellow corn kernels (about 4 ears)
- 2 cups chopped tomato
- ½ cup vertically sliced red onion
- ¼ cup finely chopped fresh basil

TO prepare dressing, combine first 6 ingredients in a jar; cover tightly and shake vigorously.

TO prepare salad, cook pasta according to package directions, omitting salt and fat. Drain and place in a large bowl. Spoon half of dressing over pasta; toss to coat.

COOL to room temperature. Add the remaining dressing, corn, tomato, onion and basil to pasta; toss to coat. Let stand 30 minutes. serves 4 (approximately 1½-cup servings)

Chef Tip: The tiny pasta soaks up the vinaigrette as it stands. Ditalini or small shells also work.

Ellen Carroll > *Apricot and Cherry Salad with lime-poppy vinaigrette*

¹/₃ cup sugar
3 tablespoons water
3 tablespoons fresh lime juice
1 teaspoon salt
1 teaspoon dry mustard
2 tablespoons vegetable oil
1 tablespoon poppy seeds

Salad
6 cups trimmed watercress
4 cups sliced apricots (about 12 medium)
3 cups halved pitted cherries

TO prepare vinaigrette, place first 5 ingredients in a blender and process until blended. Add oil and poppy seeds and process until blended.

TO prepare salad, place 1 cup watercress on each of 6 plates. Top each serving with ²/₃ cup apricot slices and ¹/₂ cup cherries. Drizzle 2 tablespoons vinaigrette over each salad. **serves 6**

Chef Tip: Sweet gold and red fruits contrast with peppery green watercress in this refreshing seasonal side salad.

Rock Shrimp
<Suzanne Somers

with citrus-serrano vinaigrette

1 red onion, sliced into thin rings
1 pound cooked rock shrimp
1 jicama, peeled and sliced into thin strips
1 recipe Citrus-Serrano Vinaigrette
1 head torn butter lettuce
1 pint cherry tomatoes

For the Citrus Serrano Vinaigrette:
1 serrano chili
2 tablespoons lemon juice
2 tablespoons lime juice
3 tablespoons chopped fresh or freeze-dried mint leaves
2 cloves garlic, chopped
Salt and freshly ground black pepper
½ cup extra-virgin olive oil

PLACE the red onion rings, cooked shrimp, and jicama into a stainless-steel or nonreactive (nonmetallic) bowl and pour the Citrus-Serrano Vinaigrette over the top. Gently toss to combine. Let mixture stand to allow flavors to develop (30 minutes is best, but it still tastes great with less marinating).

PLACE the torn butter lettuce leaves and cherry tomatoes into a salad bowl. Pour the shrimp mixture over the lettuce and toss to combine. Serve immediately. **serves 4 as an appetizer or serves 2 for lunch**

FOR the Citrus-Serrano Vinaigrette: Slice the serrano in half lengthwise and remove seeds. Finely chop the serrano or process in a mini food processor until minced. Whisk together lemon juice, lime juice, serrano, mint, garlic, salt, and pepper in a small bowl. Slowly add olive oil in a steady stream, whisking until the oil is emulsified. Taste for seasoning and adjust salt and pepper as necessary. **makes about ⅔ cup**

Chef Tip: Rock shrimp are small shrimp that have a wonderful flavor reminiscent of lobster. Rock shrimp usually come raw and peeled. They cook very quickly. Simply place in salted boiling water until they turn pink. Do not overcook or they will become tough. Remove immediately and drain.

Taco Salad Kathleen Daelemans
with chicken and white beans

1 teaspoon extra-virgin olive oil
1 pound ground chicken breast
1 teaspoon ground cumin
1 teaspoon chili powder
1 head romaine lettuce, shredded
1 mango, peeled, seeded, and diced
1 avocado, peeled, pitted, and diced
1 tomato, diced
1 medium onion, diced
1 cup peeled and shredded carrots (or half a 10-ounce bag of pre-grated carrots)
¾ cup canned white beans, rinsed and drained
½ cup scallions, diced
  Grated zest and juice of 1 lime
¼ cup store-bought salsa
¼ cup fat-free sour cream
4 pickled jalapeños
  3 to 4 servings baked tortilla chips

IN large nonstick skillet, heat olive oil over medium-high heat. Add ground chicken, cumin, and chili powder and cook for 5 to 7 minutes. Drain and transfer chicken to a large bowl.

ADD lettuce, mango, avocado, tomato, onion, carrots, beans, scallions, and lime zest and juice.

Toss until mixed well. Garnish with salsa, sour cream, jalapeños, and tortilla chips and serve. **serves 6**

Chef Tip: Ask the butcher to grind your chicken breast when you buy it to ensure you don't get ground chicken meat that has added dark meat and fat. Alternatively, cube boneless, skinless chicken breast and grind it yourself in a food processor.

Sara Foster > ## Succotash Salad
with garden tomatoes

1 pound fresh or frozen shelled
  lima beans
¼ cup olive oil
  Kernels from 2 ears fresh corn
  (1 cup fresh or frozen corn)
1 red bell pepper, cored, seeded
  and diced, or banana
  peppers, poblano peppers, or
  sweet Italian peppers
  instead of bell peppers
1 red onion, diced
1 jalapeño, cored, seeded
  and diced
2 ripe tomatoes, cored and diced
1 tablespoon fresh marjoram,
  chopped, or oregano or basil
1 tablespoon red wine vinegar
  Salt and freshly ground black
  pepper to taste

PLACE the shelled beans in large pot of boiling water. Reduce heat and simmer 10 to 15 minutes, uncovered, or until beans are crisp-tender. Drain and rinse. Set aside to cool to room temperature

HEAT the olive oil in a medium skillet. Add corn, red pepper and onion. Cook and stir over medium heat about 3 minutes, until vegetables are just tender. Add beans and jalapeño and cook 2 minutes longer, stirring occasionally.

REMOVE the skillet from the heat and add the tomatoes, marjoram and vinegar. Season with salt and pepper to taste and serve immediately or refrigerate until ready to serve. **serves 8 to 10**

Chef Tip: Try this recipe with different types of shell beans, such as speckled butter beans or black-eye, Crowder, purple hull, or field peas. This summery salad is particularly delicious with fried or barbecued chicken.

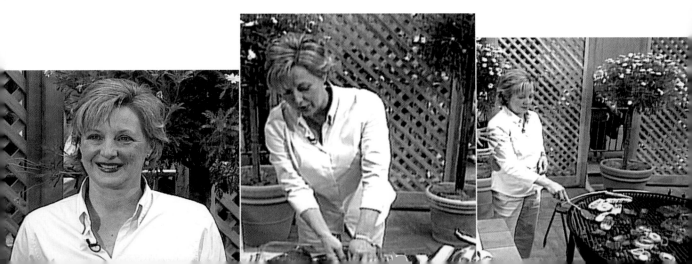

Kitchen Sink Pasta Salad Liz Weiss

1 pound dried bow tie pasta
4 to 5 cups fresh or frozen broccoli florets
1 pint cherry or grape tomatoes (about 2 cups), sliced in half
1 15½-ounce can chickpeas, drained and rinsed
1 14-ounce can artichoke hearts, drained, rinsed and quartered, optional
6 to 8 ounces feta cheese, crumbled
¾ cup pitted kalamata olives, chopped, or one 6-ounce can small black olives, drained
⅓ to ½ cup lite Italian or Caesar salad dressing
⅓ cup chopped fresh basil or cilantro, optional

COOK the pasta according to package directions. Five minutes before the pasta is done, add the broccoli. Bring the water back to a boil and cook until the pasta is done. Drain and place in a large bowl. While the pasta is still warm, add the tomatoes, chickpeas, artichoke hearts as desired, cheese, olives, salad dressing, and herbs as desired and stir to combine. Serve warm or chill for a cold salad. **serves 8 to 10**

Chef Tip: If you have school-age children, pack leftover pasta salad for a delicious and nutritious school lunch the next day.

Asian Vegetable
and chicken wrap

Cary **N**eff

½ cup finely shredded bok choy
½ cup finely shredded napa
   cabbage
2 tablespoons julienned
   water chestnuts
⅓ cup julienned carrots
¼ cup julienned shiitake
   mushrooms
4 tablespoons Sesame Dressing
   (see below)
8 ounces grilled chicken breast
2 whole wheat tortillas
¼ cup sunflower sprouts

Sesame Dressing
1 teaspoon minced fresh garlic
2 teaspoons minced fresh ginger
¼ cup rice wine vinegar
1 tablespoon tahini
   (sesame) butter
2 tablespoons low-sodium
   soy sauce
2 cups thickened vegetable stock
1 tablespoon sesame oil
½ teaspoon sriracha (chili) sauce
¼ teaspoon freshly ground
   black pepper
1 tablespoon chopped fresh
   green onions
2 teaspoons finely chopped
   cilantro

HEAT a medium sauté pan over medium high heat and add the vegetables. Stir-fry for about 1 minute and add the Sesame Dressing. Cook another 2 minutes. Remove from heat and set aside. Slice the chicken into strips and add to the vegetables and toss. Lay the tortillas on a cutting board. Divide the filling among the tortillas. Top with sunflower sprouts. Fold in the sides of the wrappers and begin folding from the bottom to form the wrap. Cut each wrap in half and serve. **serves 2**

FOR Sesame Dressing: In a blender, combine the garlic, ginger, vinegar, tahini, soy sauce, and the vegetable stock. Process until the garlic is incorporated. With the blender on low, add in the sesame oil, sriracha, and pepper. Finally add the green onions and cilantro and blend for 1 minute, just until cilantro is chopped. Season with salt to taste. **makes 3½ cups**

Chef Tip: Wrapped or unwrapped, these Asian-inspired vegetables and sauce are sure to please. Have fun and recreate the recipe into a tantalizing salad or entrée.

Liz Weiss > Confetti Chicken Wraps

- 1 tablespoon canola oil
- 1 large orange bell pepper, finely diced
- 1 pound skinless, boneless chicken breast halves, cut into bite-size pieces
- 1/2 to 1 teaspoon ground cumin
- 1/2 to 1 teaspoon chili powder
- 1 15 1/2-ounce can pinto beans, drained and rinsed
- 1 cup frozen corn kernels, thawed
- 1 cup preshredded reduced-fat Cheddar cheese
- 3/4 cup salsa
- 6 to 8 eight-inch flour tortillas
- 1/2 cup reduced-fat sour cream, optional

HEAT the oil in a large nonstick skillet over medium-high heat. Add the bell pepper and cook, stirring frequently, until tender, about 5 minutes. Add the chicken, cumin, and chili powder and cook until the chicken is no longer pink, 4 to 5 minutes. Stir in the beans, corn, cheese, and salsa and cook until the mixture is heated through and the cheese is melted, about 2 minutes. Meanwhile, stack the tortillas on a microwave-safe plate, uncovered, and heat in the microwave until warmed through, 30 to 45 seconds. Assemble by placing the chicken mixture down the center of each tortilla. Wrap burrito-style and serve with sour cream as desired. **serves 6 to 8**

Chef Tip: For families who like their food hot and fiery, add extra chili powder or use a medium or hot salsa.

Mediterranean Vegetable Wrap

Cary Neff

1 whole wheat tortilla
2 tablespoons Hummus (see below)
¼ cup julienned roasted red peppers
2 slices of tomatoes
¼ cup julienned portobella mushrooms, sautéed
¼ cup arugula
1 tablespoon finely shredded basil
2 ounces sliced fresh mozzarella cheese

Hummus

3 cups cooked chickpeas (two 15-ounce cans)
4 small garlic cloves
¼ cup lemon juice
2 teaspoon tahini (sesame) paste
1 teaspoon ground cumin
½ teaspoon sea salt
2½ teaspoons extra-virgin olive oil
½ cup water or the liquid from the cans
Paprika

PLACE the tortilla on a cutting board. Spread with the Hummus. Lay the roasted red peppers, tomatoes, mushrooms, arugula, basil, and mozzarella on top of the hummus. Fold in the sides of the wrappers and begin folding from the bottom to form the wrap.
makes: 1 wrap

FOR Hummus: Place the chickpeas, garlic, lemon juice, tahini, cumin and salt in the bowl of a food processor. Process until beans are starting to break up, about 1 minute. Add the olive oil and water. Puree until smooth and creamy. You may need to scrape down the sides to ensure all the beans are pureed. Chill for ½ hour before serving. Garnish with a sprinkle of paprika for extra flavor and color. **makes 2½ cups**

Chef Tip: Make summer a wrap with the comforting Mediterranean flavors of garbanzo beans (chickpeas), fresh arugula, basil, vine-ripened tomatoes, and a touch of mozzarella cheese. Always make extra hummus for a satisfying snack or party appetizer.

Calorie-Busting Gazpacho *with seared scallops*

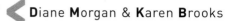

Diane **M**organ & **K**aren **B**rooks

2 large cloves garlic
1½ teaspoons sugar
¼ teaspoon cayenne pepper
1 slice day-old bread, torn into small pieces
1 bunch watercress or 3 outer romaine leaves
¼ cup rice wine or white wine vinegar
2 tablespoons olive oil
6 large fresh basil leaves
1 can (14½ ounces) beef or vegetable broth
6 medium tomatoes, cored, seeded, and cut into ¼-inch dice
2 cups V8® juice
Kosher salt and freshly ground pepper
12 fresh sea scallops, cleaned and blotted dry
2 tablespoons olive oil
Salt and freshly ground pepper
3 10-inch-long bamboo skewers, soaked in water for 30 minutes, then drained
Vegetable oil for brushing
2 tablespoons minced fresh chives

TO make the gazpacho: In a food processor or blender, puree the garlic, sugar, cayenne, and bread. As you pulse and whirl, stand up straight and tall and squeeze buns tight. (This calorie-sparing recipe can't do all the work.) Trim away any tough watercress stems, or remove the thick spines of the romaine leaves. Add the watercress or romaine to the work bowl. Add the vinegar, oil, basil, and beef or vegetable broth. Process until pureed (squeeze, two, three, four). Transfer to a large bowl and stir in the tomatoes and V8 juice. Add salt and pepper to taste. Cover and chill until ready to serve.

TO cook the scallops: Prepare a medium-hot fire in a charcoal grill or preheat a gas or electric grill on medium-high. In a bowl, toss the scallops with the olive oil and a little salt and pepper. Set aside for 15 minutes, then thread 4 scallops onto each skewer. Brush the grill grate with vegetable oil. Grill the scallops directly over medium-high heat until nicely browned outside and just opaque inside, about 2 minutes per side. Remove and slide them off the skewers.

STIR the soup and ladle into martini glasses. Feel hip, and while you're at it, move yours: Sway vigorously four times. Then garnish each glass with 2 grilled scallops and some minced chives. **serves 6**

Chef Tip: Ingredients can come and go, but the right bread is a bottom-line gazpacho ingredient. Don't even consider one of those nine-grain sprouted wheat numbers. Crusty country bread is the ticket.

Kathleen Daelemans > Swordfish *with olive oil, lemon and parsley*

1 pound skinless swordfish
   steak, cut $^3/_8$ inch thick
Coarse-grained salt and
   cracked black pepper
Grated peel of one lemon
$^1/_4$ cup loosely packed whole
   Italian parsley leaves
2 teaspoons good quality olive oil
4 lemon wedges

SEASON fish with salt and pepper. Rub both sides of fish with lemon rind. Press parsley leaves onto both sides of fish—trust me, they'll stick to the fish like postage stamps to envelopes, or at least long enough for you to get them in the pan where they'll really stick. Who cares if a few leaves fall about the pan? No one's photographing dinner.

HEAT olive oil over medium-high heat in a large nonstick skillet. When hot, but not smoking, add fish to pan and cook, turning once, until golden and fork tender, about 2 minutes per side. Serve with lemon wedges. **serves 4**

Chef Tip: This is mock pan-fried fish, the kind of fried that won't send you to the cardiac wing. Buttery swordfish steaks are my favorite fish for this quick pan supper, but this recipe will work with just about any thin fish. Remember to adjust the cooking time.

Salmon <Jacques Pépin
with spinach and tomatoes

4 cups (loosely packed)
    spinach leaves
6 boneless, skinless salmon
    fillet steaks, each about
    6 ounces and ¼ inch thick
½ cup peeled, seeded, and diced
    (½ inch) tomato
½ cup white wine
¾ teaspoon salt
½ teaspoon freshly ground
    black pepper
⅓ cup sour cream

SPREAD the spinach leaves evenly in a large skillet, and arrange the salmon fillets in a single layer on top. Add the tomato, wine, salt, and pepper, and bring to a boil. Cover and cook over medium-high heat for 3 to 4 minutes, until the salmon is barely cooked.

HEAT the oven to 180°F. Using a slotted spoon, lift the spinach from the skillet and, still holding it over the skillet, press on it to extrude most of the moisture, letting it fall back into the skillet. Transfer the spinach and fish to an ovenproof serving platter, and keep warm in the preheated oven. Reduce the juices remaining in the skillet to 4 to 5 tablespoons. Add the sour cream, bring just to the boil, and spoon over the fish. Serve immediately. **serves 6**

Chef Tip: If you can't find salmon, substitute grouper, striped bass, or another firm-fleshed fish—whatever variety is the freshest. Be sure that the thickness and size of the fish you select are about the same as what is called for at left.

Blackened Shrimp
with pomegranate-orange salsa

Ellen **C**arroll

Salsa
- 2 cups pomegranate seeds (about 4 pomegranates)
- 1 cup finely chopped orange sections (about 2 oranges)
- 1/3 cup chopped green onions
- 2 tablespoons minced, seeded jalapeño pepper
- 2 tablespoons chopped fresh cilantro
- 1/4 teaspoon salt

Shrimp
- 1 tablespoon paprika
- 2 teaspoons ground cumin
- 1 teaspoon garlic powder
- 1 teaspoon dried oregano
- 3/4 teaspoon dried thyme
- 3/4 teaspoon ground red pepper
- 1/2 teaspoon salt
- 1/2 teaspoon ground allspice
- 36 large shrimp, peeled and deveined (about 1 1/2 pounds)
- 5 teaspoons olive oil, divided

TO prepare salsa, combine the first 6 ingredients.

TO prepare shrimp, combine paprika and the next 7 ingredients (through allspice) in a large zip-top plastic bag. Add shrimp to bag; seal and shake well to coat. Remove shrimp from bag.

HEAT 2 1/2 teaspoons oil in a large nonstick skillet over medium-high heat. Add half of shrimp mixture; cook 2 minutes on each side or until done. Remove from pan. Repeat procedure with remaining 2 1/2 teaspoons oil and remaining shrimp mixture. Serve warm with salsa. **serves 12 (serving size: 3 shrimp and 1/4 cup salsa)**

Chef Tip: The jewel-toned salsa features fresh seasonal fruit and serves as a fitting complement to the shrimp, which is heavily seasoned. It also makes a nice accompaniment to grilled chicken breasts.

Liz Weiss > Chocolaty Pumpkin Bars

1 cup all-purpose flour
1 cup whole wheat flour
1 cup sugar
1 cup pecans, very finely chopped
2 teaspoons baking powder
1 teaspoon ground cinnamon
1/2 teaspoon baking soda
1/2 teaspoon salt
4 large eggs, beaten
1 15-ounce can 100%
  pure pumpkin
1/2 cup canola oil
1/4 cup 1% lowfat milk
1/2 cup mini chocolate chips

PREHEAT the oven to 350°F. Lightly oil or coat a 15×10×1-inch baking pan (jelly-roll pan) with nonstick cooking spray and set aside. Whisk together the flour, whole wheat flour, sugar, pecans, baking powder, cinnamon, baking soda, and salt in a large bowl. In a separate bowl, combine the eggs, pumpkin, canola oil, and milk. Add to the dry mixture along with the chocolate chips and stir to combine. Spread the batter evenly in the prepared pan and bake for 25 minutes or until a wooden toothpick inserted in the center comes out clean. Cool on a wire rack. **makes 30 bars**

Chef Tip: If you like, use a can of pureed sweet potatoes or squash instead of the pumpkin.

Triple Berry Pudding ◄ **K**athleen **D**aelemans

4 cups mixed berries, blueberries, raspberries, strawberries, rinsed (hull and slice strawberries)
¼ cup sugar, or to taste
1 tablespoon fresh lemon juice
6 to 8 slices stale bread (such as potato bread or challah), crusts removed

PLACE berries and sugar in a medium non-reactive saucepan over medium heat. Bring to a boil, stirring occasionally, and cook until the sugar has dissolved and berries begin to release their juices, about 10 minutes. Remove from heat, add lemon juice, and let cool to room temperature.

LINE a 9×5-inch loaf pan with plastic wrap, letting 3 inches hang over on all sides. Press plastic wrap into pan, leaving no air pockets.

TRIM bread slices to fit pan and place in a single layer on bottom. Using a slotted spoon, place a generous single layer of fruit over the bread.

DIP second layer of bread slices into pan with berries for half a minute per side to soak up excess fruit juices. Place over berry layer. Repeat with 2 more layers of fruit and bread, finishing with a layer of bread. Top with remaining juices. Finished pudding should be above the top of the pan so that when it's weighted down it will compact and absorb all the juices.

FOLD over the excess plastic wrap and cover loosely with additional plastic wrap as needed. Place loaf pan on a rimmed cookie sheet to catch any overflowing juices. Cover with a second cookie sheet and place several heavy cans on top to press and weight down the pudding. This allows the berries to release all their juices into the bread and forces the pudding to hold its shape nicely. Refrigerate 8 hours or overnight.

TO unmold, remove top layer of plastic wrap and invert onto a serving platter. Gently lift off the loaf pan and peel off the plastic wrap lining. To serve, use a serrated bread knife to cut into clean slices. **serves 6 to 8**

Chef Tip: This grand finale dessert will make a statement on any table. Serve the pudding on a large platter surrounded with sugared berries and sprigs of mint, with whipped, lightly sweetened, cream on the side. Surprisingly, this pudding is best made with potato bread or challah.

Old-Fashioned Vanilla Bread Pudding
with winter fruit

Ellen **C**arroll

1   6-inch piece vanilla bean,
      split lengthwise
1½ cups 2% low-fat milk
½   cup boiling water
½   cup chopped dried mixed fruit
¼   cup raisins
1   tablespoon margarine, melted
10 ½-inch-thick slices Italian
      bread (about 6½ ounces)
      Vegetable cooking spray
1   cup evaporated skimmed milk
½   cup sugar
⅛   teaspoon salt
⅛   teaspoon ground cinnamon
2   eggs
2   egg whites

SCRAPE seeds from vanilla bean; place the seeds and bean in a small heavy saucepan. Pour 2% low-fat milk into pan, and cook over medium-low heat to 180°F or until tiny bubbles form around edge of pan (do not boil). Remove from heat, and let cool; discard vanilla bean.

COMBINE boiling water, mixed fruit, and raisins in a small bowl; cover and let stand 30 minutes or until softened (do not drain).

BRUSH melted margarine over bread slices, and place bread on a baking sheet. Bake at 350°F for 10 minutes or until lightly toasted. Arrange half of bread in an 8-inch-square baking dish coated with cooking spray, tearing bread slices to fit dish, if needed. Spoon softened

fruit and soaking liquid over bread; top with remaining bread.

COMBINE the vanilla-milk mixture, evaporated milk, and next 5 ingredients (evaporated milk through egg whites) in a medium bowl; stir well with a wire whisk. Pour over bread, pressing gently to moisten.

COVER dish and place in a 13×9-inch baking pan; add hot water to pan to a depth of 1 inch. Bake at 350°F for 30 minutes. Uncover and bake an additional 20 minutes or until set. Serve warm. **serves 8**

Chef Tip: Using a vanilla bean is worth the cost in this recipe because it makes such a difference in the flavor. If you prefer one specific dried fruit over the mixed dried fruit, by all means experiment.

Cary Neff > Lemon Raspberry Cookies

¾ cup butter
1 cup evaporated raw cane sugar
1 large egg
3 large egg whites
¼ cup lemon juice
1 teaspoon lemon zest
3½ cups unbleached flour
1 teaspoon baking soda
⅓ cup white chocolate chips
½ cup raspberries

PREHEAT oven to 350°F; lightly spray cookie sheet with oil and set aside.

CREAM together the butter and sugar. Add the egg and egg whites in stages. Mix in the lemon juice and zest. Combine the flour and baking soda. Mix the dry ingredients into the batter. Mix in the white chocolate chips. Fold in the raspberries.

PORTION the cookies by the teaspoon and bake in the 350°F oven. Bake for 7 to 10 minutes. **makes 60 cookies (60 servings)**

Ginger Spice Cookies < Cary Neff

³/₄	cup butter
¹/₂	cup prune puree
¹/₂	cup pumpkin puree
1	cup molasses
¹/₄	cup egg whites
1¹/₂	cups unbleached all-purpose flour
1	cup whole wheat pastry flour
1	teaspoon baking soda
1¹/₄	teaspoons ground ginger
1	teaspoon cinnamon
¹/₂	teaspoon ground cloves
¹/₂	teaspoon nutmeg

PREHEAT oven to 350°F; lightly spray cookie sheet with oil and set aside.

IN mixing bowl add butter; cream until soft. Add prune puree and pumpkin and mix well. Add molasses and egg whites; beat until creamy. Stir dry ingredients into wet mixture and mix until well incorporated. Portion the cookies by the teaspoon and bake in a 350°F oven. Bake for 12 to 15 minutes. **makes 65 cookies (65 servings)**

Chef Tip: Conscious Cuisine® utilizes fruit purees and least processed flours to create scrumptious cookies that delight with goodness.

Strawberry Sherbet ◄ **A**lice **W**aters

2 **1-pint baskets of local, organic
strawberries (about 4 cups)**
¾ **cup water**
½ **cup sugar**
**A few drops of lemon juice
or kirsch (optional)**

RINSE, dry and hull the very ripe strawberries. Puree them with the water and sugar. Taste and adjust the flavor with more sugar or with a few drops of lemon juice or kirsch if needed.

FREEZE according to the instructions for your ice cream maker. **makes about 1 quart**

Chef Tip: Although some seeds in the sherbet are desirable, consider straining out half of the seeds from the puree.

two

Gourmet Feasts

Matt Lauer >

Q&A

Q. Who inspired your interest in cooking?

A. My mother was always a good cook, not fancy, just good meals that brought the family together. Her pot roast and potato pancakes meal was always my favorite.

Q. What is your first memory of cooking?

A. When I was a bachelor, I really dove into cooking. I would buy the large (economy) size cans of Beefaroni®, tear the label off the can, open it, and put the can right on the burner of the stove; then I would stir it with a large spoon, and when it was hot, I would pick it up with a pot holder. When it was ready, I would eat it right out of the can, so the only thing I ever had to wash was the spoon! Now that's cooking!

Q. Since you have traveled across the globe, what is your favorite regional cuisine?

A. The best part of my job is that I have been able to go to just about every region of the world. I'm a huge fan of northern Italian cooking and also love Lebanese cooking.

Q. What meals do you make for your kids?

A. I make a mean scrambled egg.

Q. What is your favorite gourmet meal to eat or prepare?

A. I actually made duck confit one day. To be honest, I should say one weekend because it seemed like it took that long to complete the recipe, but when it was done it was fabulous. Even my wife, who usually feigns illness when I go near the kitchen, said it was fantastic!

Q. What are your favorite spices for cooking?

A. Salt and pepper. I'm a simple guy with simple tastes.

Q. What do you make when you are entertaining guests? Why?

A. I make drinks so dinner takes on less importance.

Q. What is your favorite comfort food? What do you like to prepare when you are just cooking casually?

A. Steak is my comfort food. I am the furthest thing from a

vegetarian. I'm a carnivore, and when I get stressed out, get me a porterhouse!

Q. What is the food that you should not eat but do?

A. Ice cream. At one point in my life I would make a milk shake with a pint of Häagen Dazs® every night, preferably coffee or chocolate.

Q. Do you follow recipes or do you just like to experiment? Is cooking a creative process for you?

A. I go by the book. Experimenting is dangerous with me.

Q. What do you eat for breakfast before the show?

A. I tend to "graze" during the show, a little cereal here, a muffin there, some egg salad with crackers in the middle of the morning.

Pasta with Sausage ◀ Matt Lauer
and broccoli rabe

1 pound hot or sweet Italian sausage links
1 tablespoon olive oil
8 ounces broccoli rabe, coarsely chopped (6 cups)
1 large leek, cut into ¼-inch slices (½ cup)
2 cloves garlic, minced
⅔ cup chicken broth
½ cup purchased roasted red sweet peppers, drained and cut into thin bite-size strips
6 ounces dried penne pasta
¼ cup snipped fresh basil
½ teaspoon cracked black pepper
⅓ cup finely shredded Parmesan cheese

FILL a 12-inch skillet with ½ inch of water. Bring to boiling. Add sausage links. Cook, covered, for 15 minutes; drain. Remove sausage links to a cutting board. Cut sausage links in ½-inch slices. Return sausage slices to skillet and cook in hot oil over medium-high heat for 2 to 3 minutes or until brown; remove from pan.

ADD broccoli rabe, leek, and garlic to skillet. Cook, stirring until broccoli rabe is wilted and leek is tender. Stir in sausage, chicken broth, and roasted sweet peppers. Bring to boiling; reduce heat.

COVER and simmer gently for 2 to 3 minutes or until broccoli rabe is crisp-tender.

MEANWHILE, cook pasta according to package directions; drain. Add cooked pasta, basil, and black pepper to sausage mixture; toss gently to combine. Top with Parmesan cheese. **serves 4**

Ensalada Mexicana <Aaron Sanchez
(market salad)

1 chile de árbol, stemmed
   and seeded (see Chef Tip)
2 small cucumbers, peeled
   and seeded
½ pound jicama, peeled
1 mango, peeled and cut
   into chunks
   Juice of 2 limes
   Salt and freshly ground pepper
1 avocado, pitted, peeled
   and sliced
¼ cup extra-virgin olive oil

IN a dry cast-iron skillet, toast the chile over medium-low heat for 2 minutes, until fragrant, turn it and shake the pan so it doesn't scorch. Put the toasted chile in a clean coffee grinder or spice mill and grind into a powder.

CUT the cucumbers and jicama into 2-inch-long, ⅛-inch matchsticks and add to a mixing bowl with the mango and lime juice. Toss to combine and season with salt and pepper to taste. Pile the mixture onto serving plates and drizzle with the juices in the bottom of the bowl. Fan the avocado slices on top of the salad and sprinkle with a fair amount of chile powder. Drizzle with the oil and serve. **serves 4**

Chef Tip: Chile de árbol gets its name from the Spanish word for "tree" (arbol) because these chiles grow hanging from trees or small bushes. This small chile measures about 2 to 3 inches long, is scarlet red, and adds a smoky, grassy flavor backed with an acidic heat. Chile de árbol is often used to flavor oils and vinegars.

Aaron Sanchez > Chilled Yellow Tomato Soup *with aji amarillo*

Olive oil
2 pounds of ripe yellow tomatoes
   (about 6 to 8 large tomatoes)
6 cloves of garlic (thinly sliced)
½ cup of white wine vinegar
1 whole aji amarillo or two
   tablespoons of aji amarillo
   paste
3 fresh basil leaves
   (sliced paper thin)
For garnish: melon balls of
   cantaloupe, cucumber, jicama

BEGIN in a large sauce pot with a tablespoon of good olive oil and begin lightly cooking the garlic for about 3 minutes until the oil has been perfumed, making sure not to brown the garlic.

THEN add the tomatoes, vinegar, aji amarillo chile and stir well. Cook over a medium heat for about 15 minutes, then remove from the heat.

PUREE the soup in a food processor or blender and then chill in the refrigerator for 30 minutes. Season with salt and pepper and serve garnished with basil, cucumber, melon and jicama. **serves 4**

Mushroom Fricasse < **M**ario **B**atali

4 tablespoons (¹/₂ stick) butter
¹/₂ cup thinly sliced morel or
 chanterelle mushrooms
¹/₂ cup thinly sliced shiitake
 mushrooms
¹/₂ cup thinly sliced portobello
 mushrooms
¹/₂ cup thinly sliced domestic
 mushrooms
¹/₄ cup tomato paste
 Pinch ground cinnamon
 Pinch ground nutmeg
 Pinch ground cloves
 Salt and pepper

IN a large skillet, melt the butter over medium heat. Add all of the sliced mushrooms and sauté until just beginning to brown. Add the tomato paste and stir to incorporate.

SEASON, to taste, with cinnamon, nutmeg, cloves, salt, and pepper.
serves 4

Nice-Style Stuffed Vegetables ◄ Colman Andrews

3 small eggplants
6 small green or red bell peppers
½ cup extra-virgin olive oil
Salt
3 small yellow onions, peeled
3 small zucchini
3 medium tomatoes
¼ pound lean salt pork, diced
½ pound ground lamb
¾ cup cooked rice
1 cup finely chopped fresh
   flat-leaf parsley
2 cloves garlic, peeled
   and minced
Freshly ground black pepper
2 eggs, lightly beaten
½ cup finely grated Parmigiano-
   Reggiano
½ cup fresh bread crumbs
1 bunch fresh thyme

PREHEAT oven to 350°F. Cut eggplants in half lengthwise. Cut tops from peppers, then core and seed them. Place eggplants and peppers in an oiled baking sheet and brush lightly with oil. Bake for 30 minutes, then remove from oven and set aside to cool. When eggplants are cool enough to handle, scoop out pulp, leaving about ½-inch-thick shell. Chop pulp finely and set aside in a large bowl.

HEAT a large pot of salted water over medium heat. Add onions and zucchini and simmer for about 10 minutes. Drain and set aside to cool.

HALVE onions crosswise and remove centers, leaving a shell of about 3 outer layers. Halve zucchini lengthwise and scoop out pulp, leaving about ½-inch-thick shell. Halve tomatoes crosswise, then squeeze out and discard seeds and juice. Scoop pulp from tomatoes,

finely chop and add to eggplant pulp. Finely chop onion centers and zucchini pulp and add them to eggplant mixture as well. Increase oven temperature to 375°F. Heat 2 tablespoons oil in a large pan over low heat. Stir in vegetable mixture, salt pork, lamb, rice, parsley, and garlic. Season to taste with salt and pepper. Cook for about 15 minutes, stirring occasionally. Remove from heat, cool slightly, then stir in eggs.

FILL vegetable shells (don't pack too tightly), top with Parmigiano-Reggiano and bread crumbs, drizzle with remaining olive oil and bake for 30 minutes on an oiled baking sheet. Serve garnished with fresh thyme sprigs. **serves 6**

Chef Tip: For a quick and efficient way to chop a tangly bunch of parsley, gather the parsley leaves into a tight mound on a cutting board with one hand and finely chop leaves with a large sharp kitchen knife. Continue chopping parsley to desired fineness.

Nobu Matsuhisa > Black Cod with Miso

4 black cod fillets, about
   $1/2$ pound each
3 cups Nobu-style Saikyo Miso
   (see below)

Nobu-Style Saikyo Miso
$3/4$ cup sake
$3/4$ cup mirin
2 cups white miso paste
$1 1/4$ cups granulated sugar

PAT the fillets thoroughly dry with paper towels. Slather the fish with Nobu-style Saikyo Miso and place in a non-reactive dish or bowl and cover tightly with plastic wrap. Leave to steep in the refrigerator for 2 to 3 days.

PREHEAT oven to 400°F. Preheat a grill or broiler. Lightly wipe off any excess miso clinging to the fillets but don't rinse it off. Place the fish on the grill, or in a boiler pan, and grill or broil until the surface of the fish turns brown. Then bake for 10 to 15 minutes.

ARRANGE the black cod fillets on individual plates. Add a few extra drops of Nobu-style Saikyo Miso to each plate. **serves 4**

FOR Nobu-style Saikyo Miso: Bring the sake and mirin to a boil in medium saucepan over high heat. Boil for 20 seconds to evaporate the alcohol. Turn the heat down to low and add the miso paste, mixing with a wooden spoon. When the miso has dissolved completely, turn the heat up to high again and add the sugar, stirring constantly with the wooden spoon to ensure that the bottom of the pan doesn't burn. Remove from heat once the sugar is fully dissolved. Cool to room temperature.

Chef Tip: This recipe also works for beef, toro, and salmon.

Squid Pasta < Nobu Matsuhisa
with light garlic sauce

4 broccoli florets, cut into
    bite-size pieces
    Sea salt
4¼ ounces fresh mongo cuttlefish,
    cleaned and prepared
    Freshly ground black pepper
4 teaspoons clarified butter
1 clove garlic, thinly sliced
4 shittake mushrooms,
    stems removed
6 spears green asparagus,
    cut into 2-inch lengths
4 tablespoons Sake Soy Sauce
    (see below)
    Shichimi togarashi to taste

Sake Soy Sauce
¾ cup sake
5 tablespoons soy sauce

BOIL the broccoli for 1½ minutes in a small pot of boiling water to which a pinch of sea salt has been added. Plunge briefly into iced water and drain.

PAT the cuttlefish dry with paper towels. Cut the body horizontally into 2-inch-wide strips. Use a knife to make fine vertical incisions down the length of each strip along the grain. These should be fairly deep but very close together. (When the cuttlefish cooks and curls, the incisions will give it a conchiglie-like texture.) Cut the cuttlefish parallel to the incisions in ½-inch-wide strips. Sprinkle the strips with a little sea salt and black pepper.

HEAT a medium frying pan over medium heat. Add the clarified butter and sauté the garlic slices. When the aroma of the garlic has been released, turn the heat up to high, add the shiitake mushrooms and fry lightly. Add the cuttlefish,

green asparagus and broccoli, in that order, and season with a little sea salt and black pepper.

WHEN the cuttlefish is about 70% cooked (the surface turns opaque), add the Sake Soy Sauce in a swirling motion just before turning off the heat. Mix the contents of the pan to distribute the sauce evenly. Place in a serving dish. Add shichimi togarashi to taste. **serves 6**

FOR Sake Soy Sauce: Bring the sake to a boil in a saucepan and take off heat as soon as its alcohol content has evaporated and mix with soy sauce.

Chef Tip: Shichimi togarashi, or seven-spice mixture, is a snappy collection of seven dried and ground flavors.

Valencian Paella *with shellfish* ◀ **C**olman **A**ndrews

2 pounds chicken, cut into small
  serving pieces
  Olive oil
¼ pint chicken stock
12 mussels, cleaned (see note*)
8 ounces prawns and/or small
  shrimp, heads and shells on
8 to 12 ounces assorted white
  beans, butter beans and
  broad beans or green beans,
  cooked and drained
1 tomato, seeded and grated
  (see note**) or peeled,
  seeded and chopped
1 tablespoon sweet paprika
6 to 8 threads saffron,
  lightly toasted
1⅓ pounds short-grain rice
  Salt

IN paella, cassola, or other wide, flat-bottom pan, sauté the chicken pieces in a small amount of oil until golden-brown; then remove them, drain and set aside. Meanwhile, bring stock to a boil; then reduce the heat and simmer. Pour off excess fat from the paella; then add the mussels and prawns and beans, tomato and paprika, and stir well.

ADD the stock, return chicken to a pan and simmer for 10 minutes; then crumble saffron into pan, and salt to taste.

STIR in the rice; then cook over a medium-high flame without stirring for 20 to 25 minutes or until the rice is done and the liquid has evaporated. (Do not allow the rice to burn; a dark brown crust on the bottom and sides of the pan, however, is desirable.)

WHEN paella is finished, carefully arrange the mussels and prawns on top of the rice, using tongs and being careful not to leave the rice uneven (top should be flat); then let stand 5 to 10 minutes off heat before serving. **serves 8 to 10 as appetizer or 6 to 8 as main course.**

*Note: To clean mussels, rinse them under running water, brushing if necessary with a small stiff brush, then pull off the "beards" and discard. Place the mussels in a large bowl with cold water to cover. Stir them around briefly with your hands, letting them knock together, then let soak for about 10 minutes. Remove mussels from the bowl. If there is sand at the bottom of the bowl, repeat the process, continuing until no sand remains.

**Note: To grate tomatoes, slice a whole unpeeled tomato in half horizontally, squeeze out the seeds, and then grate the fruit on the large holes of a four-sided grater, flattening it out with the palm of your hand as you go, stopping when the peel is about to reach the holes. The result is a sort of instant coarse puree.

Chef Tip: It's important to use only short- or round-grain rice, not the long-grain variety called for in so many British paella and "Spanish rice" recipes. Valencian rice is sometimes available; if you can't find it, substitute Italian arborio (as for risotto).

Mario Batali > Stuffed Onions
(cipolle ripiene)

8 large red onions
Salt and pepper
4 tablespoons extra-virgin olive
oil, plus 4 tablespoons
¾ pound ground beef chuck
½ cup freshly grated caciocavallo
4 tablespoons fresh marjoram
leaves
½ cup dry red wine
¾ cup plus ½ cup fresh
bread crumbs

PREHEAT oven to 425°F. Carefully cut the onions exactly in half across the equator, remove the peel, and slice the smallest amount from the point end so that the halves will stand upright on the point end. Place the halves upright on a cookie sheet, season with salt and pepper, and drizzle with 4 tablespoons oil. Bake until just softened, about 15 minutes. Remove and dig out the center of each half with a spoon to leave the last ¼-inch around the perimeter and base. Chop them and set the removed onion bits aside for later.

IN a 12- to 14-inch sauté pan, heat the remaining 4 tablespoons oil over medium heat until smoking. Add the ground chuck and cook until fat has rendered and meat has started to brown, about 20 to 25 minutes.

DRAIN the fat, add the removed pieces of onions, and continue cooking until the onions are very soft, 10 to 12 minutes.

REMOVE the meat mixture from the heat and place in a bowl. Add the caciocavallo, marjoram, red wine, and ¾ cup of the bread crumbs, stir to mix well, and season with salt and pepper. Stuff each of the onion halves carefully just over the edge of each and sprinkle with remaining bread crumbs. Place onions in a well-oiled glass baking pan, drizzle with extra-virgin olive oil, and place in the oven. Cook until dark golden brown on top, about 20 to 25 minutes, and serve. **serves 8**

Picadillo < Aaron Sanchez

1 tablespoon olive oil
2 pounds lean ground beef
½ cup chopped white onion
½ cup diced red bell pepper
½ cup diced yellow bell pepper
½ tablespoon of chopped garlic
3 bay leaves
1 teaspoon of toasted
  ground cumin
¼ cup sliced green olives
¼ cup sliced toasted almonds
¼ cup golden raisins
¾ cup tomato paste
¼ cup chopped parsley

BEGIN by heating a medium Dutch oven over high heat. Add a tablespoon of olive oil and the ground beef. Be sure to distribute the beef evenly throughout the pan. Allow beef to brown on the bottom by not moving it for 5 minutes. As the meat begins to lose its red tint, start mixing in the onions, peppers, garlic, bay leaves and cumin. Let it cook for 7 minutes until the vegetables become translucent. Then add the olives, almonds, raisins, tomato paste and parsley. Be sure to mix it thoroughly with a spoon so that the tomato paste is well incorporated. Season to taste with salt and pepper. **serves 4**

Chicken Satay ◄ **D**aniel **B**oulud
with spicy peanut sauce

For the Sauce:
- 2 tablespoons vegetable oil
- 2 shallots
- 1 clove garlic, finely chopped
- 1 small jalapeño chile, halved, seeded, and finely chopped
- 1 cup plus 3 tablespoons creamy peanut butter
- 1/2 cup unsweetened coconut milk
- 1 tablespoon Asian fish sauce (preferably nuoc nam)
- 2 tablespoons tamarind pulp or paste
- 2 teaspoons honey

For the Chicken:
- 1 tablespoon coriander seeds
- 2 teaspoons fennel seeds
- 1 stalk lemongrass, trimmed, outer leaves removed, and bulb thinly sliced
- 2 cloves garlic, finely chopped
- 2 tablespoons soy sauce
- 1 tablespoon Asian sesame oil Freshly squeezed juice of 1/2 lime
- 2 teaspoons sugar
- 1/2 teaspoon turmeric
- 1/2 teaspoon salt
- 1 whole skinless, boneless chicken breast (about 3/4 pound)
- 16 8-inch bamboo skewers, soaked in water for 30 minutes

TO prepare the sauce: Warm the vegetable oil in a small skillet over medium heat. Add the shallots, garlic, and chile and cook, while stirring, until the shallots are tender and translucent, about 5 minutes. Reduce the heat to low and add the peanut butter, coconut milk, fish sauce, tamarind, and honey. Mix well; cook for 30 minutes, stirring occasionally.

TRANSFER to a blender and purée until smooth. (The sauce can be prepared up to 1 day ahead and stored in an airtight container in the refrigerator. Just before serving, rewarm the sauce.)

TO prepare the chicken: Put the coriander and fennel seeds in a small skillet over medium heat and cook, shaking the pan back and forth occasionally until toasted and fragrant, about 5 minutes. Finely grind in a spice grinder. Mix together the lemongrass, garlic,

soy sauce, sesame oil, lime juice, ground coriander and fennel, sugar, turmeric, and salt. Pour about one-third of the mixture into a shallow baking dish. Cut the chicken lengthwise into sixteen 1/4-inch-thick slices and arrange them on top of the lemongrass mixture in a single layer in the dish. Pour the remaining marinade on top. Cover and refrigerate overnight. Gently scrape the marinade off the chicken using the back of a knife. Thread a chicken slice onto each skewer. Heat a grill pan over medium-high heat until hot. Cook the chicken 1 1/2 to 2 minutes on each side. Serve immediately with the peanut sauce. **serves 4**

Chef Tip: Serve with 2001 Domaine du Clos Naudin, a Vouvray demi-sec. The clean tropical fruit flavors and midrange acidity are soft on the palate while echoing the richness of the peanut sauce.

Jacques **Pépin** > # Poulet à la Crème
(chicken with cream sauce)

1 tablespoon unsalted butter
1 chicken (about 3 pounds),
   cut into 4 pieces (2 legs and
   2 breasts, with bones)
½ teaspoon salt, plus more to taste
¼ teaspoon freshly ground black
   pepper, plus more to taste
½ cup fruity white wine (I used
   Macon white, a Chardonnay)
½ cup good chicken stock
1 small onion (about 3 ounces),
   peeled and left whole
1 bouquet garni, made of a dozen
   sprigs of parsley, 2 bay
   leaves, 2 sprigs of thyme, all
   tied together with string
1 tablespoon unsalted butter,
   at room temperature
1 tablespoon all-purpose flour
1 cup heavy cream

MELT the tablespoon of butter in a sturdy saucepan, and add the 4 pieces of chicken, skin side down. Sprinkle the chicken with the salt and pepper, and brown over medium heat, turning, for about 10 minutes. The chicken should be lightly browned, with the skin a blond rather than a dark brown color. Remove and discard some of the rendered fat, leaving only 1 to 2 tablespoons in the pan.

ADD the wine, chicken stock, onion, and bouquet garni. Bring to a boil, and boil gently, covered, for 20 to 25 minutes, or until the chicken is tender. Transfer the chicken to a platter, and discard the onion and bouquet garni. Boil the liquid in the pan until it is reduced to about ¾ cup.

MEANWHILE, make a beurre manié, or kneaded butter, by whisking together the tablespoon of soft butter and the flour in a small bowl. Pick up this mixture on the looped wires of a whisk, and whisk it into the reduced liquid in the pan until the mixture is smooth. Bring to a boil to thicken the liquid, then add the cream, return to a boil, and boil gently for 5 minutes. While the sauce is boiling, you may want to remove the bones from the breast and leg pieces of the chicken, leaving the thigh, drumstick, and wing bones in place. Arrange the chicken on a serving platter.

TASTE the sauce, and add salt and pepper if needed. Strain the sauce through a fine sieve held over the chicken, and serve immediately.
serves 4

Chef Tip: With the addition of 1 tablespoon of chopped fresh tarragon, this dish becomes poulet à l'estragon. The chicken is conventionally cut into four pieces and cooled with the bones in, which keeps the meat from drying out.

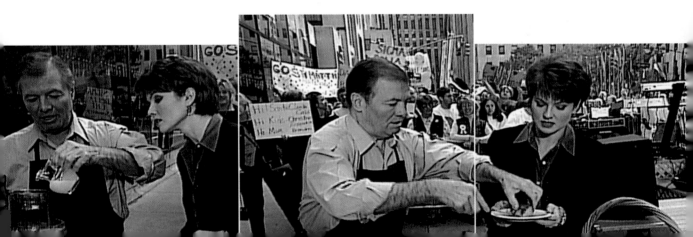

Lamb Stew
with rosemary and orange

Daniel Boulud

4 to 6 tablespoons extra-virgin olive oil
1 4-pound lamb shoulder, boned and cut into 1-inch chunks
Salt and freshly ground pepper
1 large onion, cut into 1/2-inch-thick wedges
4 small carrots, cut into 1/2-inch-thick slices
2 large turnips, peeled and diced into 1/2-inch cubes, or 16 baby turnips, peeled and trimmed
1 large celery root, peeled and diced into 1/2-inch cubes
1 medium fennel bulb, trimmed and cut into 6 wedges
3 cloves garlic, coarsely chopped
1 teaspoon finely chopped rosemary leaves
1 3-inch cinnamon stick
1/4 cup all-purpose flour
2 tablespoons tomato paste
1 teaspoon finely chopped flat-leaf parsley leaves
Freshly squeezed juice of 1 orange
1/2 cup dry white wine
5 to 6 cups water or unsalted chicken stock
4 plum tomatoes, peeled, seeded and diced into 1/2-inch cubes
1/2 teaspoon finely grated orange zest

CENTER a rack in the oven and preheat the oven to 300°F. Warm 2 tablespoons of olive oil in a Dutch oven or large pot over high heat. Season the lamb with salt and pepper. Sear the meat on all sides until golden brown, 10 to 15 minutes. Transfer the lamb to a plate. Add 2 tablespoons of the oil to the pot and reduce the heat to medium-high. Add the onion, carrots, turnips, celery root, fennel, garlic, rosemary and cinnamon stick. Season with salt and pepper and cook, while stirring, until the vegetables soften, 10 to 12 minutes. Add the lamb and cook, while stirring, for 6 to 8 minutes, adding more olive oil if needed.

SPRINKLE the flour on top and continue to cook, while stirring, for 5 minutes. Stir in the tomato paste and parsley. Add the orange juice and wine and cook until the liquid is reduced by half. Add enough water to almost cover the lamb and vegetables; bring to a boil. Add the tomatoes and orange zest; cover the pot. Bake 60 to 75 minutes until the lamb is fork-tender. Serve immediately. **serves 4**

Chef Tip: The very affordable Dr. Cosimo Taurino's Notarpanaro, a peppery Italian wine, is a great match. Another option comes from California. Infused with the penetrating aromas of spices and cassis, Ravenswood Zinfandel, Vintner's Blend, is also characterized by its smoked-meat and dried-fruit flavors.

Roast Leg of Lamb Stuffed *with Italian white beans and spinach*

Sara **F**oster

1 cup dry cannellini beans or
  navy beans, rinsed and picked
  over, or 2 cups canned navy
  or cannellini beans that have
  been rinsed and drained
6 tablespoons olive oil
6 cloves garlic, peeled and
  smashed with flat side of knife
8 cups firmly packed spinach,
  washed, drained and
  stems removed
1 4^{1}/$_{2}$- to 5-pound boneless leg
  of lamb, trimmed of excess
  fat and silver skin
^{1}/$_{2}$ cup dry red wine
1 tablespoon freshly ground
  black pepper
1 teaspoon kosher salt
1 tablespoon chopped fresh
  rosemary leaves or
  1 tablespoon dried rosemary

PREHEAT oven to 425°F.

PLACE the beans in about 6 cups of water and bring to a boil. Cook until tender, about 1 hour. Drain, rinse and set aside to cool. (Note: If using canned beans, omit this step, and proceed directly to next step.)

HEAT 2 tablespoons of the olive oil in a large skillet over medium heat. Add 3 cloves of the garlic and cook and stir for 1 to 2 minutes. Add the spinach and cook 1 to 2 minutes, until just wilted, stirring constantly. Remove from the heat and set aside to cool.

LAY the lamb fat-side-down on a cutting board or other work surface. Spread about ^{1}/$_{2}$ cup beans and ^{1}/$_{2}$ cup of the spinach-garlic mixture evenly over the center part of the surface. Reserve remaining beans and spinach.

ROLL the leg up lengthwise into a log and tie with kitchen twine. Place in a baking dish.

MAKE several slits in the fat of the lamb and stuff the remaining garlic into the slits. Coat the outside of the lamb with wine,

2 tablespoons olive oil, pepper, salt and rosemary.

HEAT the remaining 2 tablespoons of olive oil in a large ovenproof skillet or Dutch oven and brown the rolled lamb evenly on all sides, about 10 minutes total. Add the wine marinade to the pan and roast 55 minutes to 1 hour for medium rare (about 12 minutes per pound) or until meat thermometer registers 130° to 135°F (140° to 145°F for medium, about 1 hour 10 to 15 minutes) when inserted into the thickest part of the leg. Baste lamb with pan juices several times during the cooking process. Remove the lamb from the oven, cover loosely and let the lamb rest about 10 minutes before carving.

REMOVE twine, place lamb on a carving board and slice lamb into ^{1}/$_{4}$- to ^{1}/$_{2}$-inch slices. Reheat the reserved cooked navy beans and wilted spinach and serve alongside the lamb. **serves 6 to 8**

Chef Tip: Try different types of greens in this recipe in place of the spinach. I like to use turnip greens, kale, or collard greens. It is also really great made with lentils in place of the white beans.

Mario Batali > Veal Chops Pizzaiolo

4 tablespoons extra-virgin
   olive oil, plus 2 tablespoons
   Spanish onion, cut into
   ¼-inch dice
2 tablespoons dried oregano
1 cup Basic Tomato Sauce,
   recipe follows
¼ cup water
4 loin or rib veal chops, about
   ¾ pound each
1 pound fresh mozzarella
8 leaves fresh basil

PREHEAT broiler to 500°F. In a
2- to 3-quart saucepan, heat
4 tablespoons oil until smoking.
Add the onion and oregano and
cook 7 to 9 minutes, until the onion
is soft and light golden brown. Add
basic tomato sauce and ¼ cup
water, and bring to a boil.

REDUCE heat, simmer 10 minutes,
and set aside just off of the burner

to keep warm. Season the veal
chops with salt and pepper, sauté
in remaining 2 tablespoons of olive
oil until light golden brown. Turn
and cook on other side to desired
doneness, about 7 to 9 minutes
for medium-rare. Spoon 3 to
4 tablespoons of the warm tomato
sauce over each chop, leaving the
bone exposed. Grate the mozzarella
on the widest part of the cheese
grater and sprinkle over the chops.
Place the cookie sheet with the
chops under the broiler again and
cook until cheese is bubbling and
golden brown, about 2 to 3 minutes.

REMOVE from the broiler to the
platter, tear the basil leaves and
sprinkle over the chops, and serve
immediately. **serves 4**

Basic Tomato Sauce:
¼ cup extra-virgin olive oil
1 Spanish onion, chopped in
   ¼-inch dice
4 garlic cloves, peeled and
   thinly sliced
3 tablespoons chopped
   fresh thyme leaves, or
   1 tablespoon dried
½ medium carrot, finely shredded
2 (28-ounce) cans peeled whole
   tomatoes, crushed by hand
   and juices reserved
   Salt

IN a 3-quart saucepan, heat the
olive oil over medium heat. Add the
onion and garlic and cook until soft
and light golden brown, about 8 to
10 minutes. Add the thyme and
carrot and cook 5 minutes more,
until the carrot is quite soft. Add
the tomatoes and juice and bring to
a boil, stirring often. Lower the
heat and simmer for 30 minutes
until as thick as hot cereal. Season
with salt and serve. This sauce
holds one week in the refrigerator,
or up to 6 months in the freezer.

Rosemary Braised Veal Shank

‹ **D**aniel **B**oulud

1 veal shank, about 2 pounds (ask your butcher to trim the top and bottom bones)
1 tablespoon salt
1/2 teaspoon freshly ground pepper
4 sprigs rosemary, cut to the same length as the shank
5 tablespoons extra-virgin olive oil
2 large Spanish onions, peeled, trimmed and cut into 1/2-inch-thick wedges
6 cloves garlic, peeled and sliced
4 stalks celery, peeled, trimmed and cut on the bias into 1/2-inch-thick slices
2 large carrots, peeled, trimmed, and cut on the bias into 1/2-inch-thick slices
1 leek, white and light green parts only, sliced, washed, and cut on the bias into 1/2-inch-thick slices
1 tablespoon tomato paste
1 tablespoon whole black peppercorns, crushed
2 bay leaves
1/2 tablespoon all-purpose flour
2 cups dry white wine
8 cups unsalted beef stock or store-bought low-sodium beef broth
1 large tomato, peeled, seeded, and cut into 1/2-inch cubes

CENTER a rack in the oven and preheat the oven to 350°F.

SEASON the shank with the salt and pepper. Use kitchen twine to tie the shank in 1-inch intervals. Tuck in the rosemary sprigs.

WARM 3 tablespoons of the olive oil in a Dutch oven or casserole over high heat. Slip the meat into the pan and brown it evenly, turning it carefully as needed until all the surfaces of the meat are a light golden brown. Transfer the shank to a platter and let rest. Warm the remaining 2 tablespoons olive oil in the same pan over medium heat. Add the onions, garlic, celery, carrots, and leek and cook until the vegetables are tender but have no color, approximately 8 to 10 minutes. Add the tomato paste,

peppercorns, and bay leaves and cook for 2 minutes. Stir in the flour, then add the wine, stock, tomato, and the shank. Bring the liquid to a boil and cover the pot with a lid. Slide it into the oven to braise until the shank is very tender, about 2 1/2 hours.

TRANSFER the meat to a heated serving platter. Cut off and discard the kitchen twine and rosemary. Boil the pan liquid until it reduces by three-quarters. Strain the sauce over the meat and serve immediately. **serves 6**

Chef Tip: Serve with Santa Maria Valley Pinot Noir, California (U.S.), Byron 1998. This light-bodied wine, with cinnamon and red-berry aromas, pairs well with the carrots and turnips. The vivacious nature of the wine with high acidity enlivens the slowly braised veal shank.

Short Ribs Braised in Red Wine ◀ **D**aniel **B**oulud

3 bottles dry red wine
8 short ribs, trimmed of excess fat
2 tablespoons vegetable oil
 Salt
1 teaspoon black peppercorns, crushed
 Flour for dredging
10 cloves garlic, peeled
8 large shallots, peeled, trimmed and split
2 medium carrots, peeled, trimmed and cut into 1-inch lengths
2 stalks celery, peeled, trimmed and cut into 1-inch lengths
1 medium leek, white and light green parts only, trimmed, coarsely chopped, washed and dried
6 sprigs parsley
2 sprigs thyme
2 bay leaves
2 tablespoons tomato paste
3 quarts unsalted beef stock or store-bought low-sodium beef broth
 Freshly ground white pepper

POUR the wine into a large saucepan set over medium heat. When the wine is hot, carefully set it aflame, let the flames die out, then increase the heat so that the wine boils; allow it to boil until it cooks down by half. Remove from the heat.

CENTER a rack in the oven and preheat the oven to 350°F. Warm the oil in a Dutch oven or large casserole over medium-high heat. Season the ribs all over with salt and crushed pepper. Dust half the ribs with about 1 tablespoon flour and then, when the oil is hot, slip the ribs into the pot and sear 4 to 5 minutes on a side, until the ribs are well browned. Transfer the browned ribs to a plate, dust the remaining ribs with flour, and sear in the same manner. Remove all but 1 tablespoon of fat from the pot, lower the heat under the pot to medium, and toss in the vegetables and herbs. Brown the vegetables lightly, for 5 to 7 minutes, then stir in the tomato paste and cook for 1 minute to blend.

ADD the reduced wine, browned ribs and stock to the pot. Bring to

the boil, cover the pot closely, and slide it into the oven to braise 2½ hours, or until the ribs are tender enough to be easily pierced with a fork. Every 30 minutes or so, lift the lid and skim and discard whatever fat may have bubbled up to the surface. (Not only can you make this a day in advance, it's best to make the recipe up to this point, cool and chill the ribs and stock in the pan, and, on the next day, scrape off the fat. Rewarm before continuing.)

CAREFULLY (the tender meat falls apart easily) transfer the meat to a heated serving platter with raised rims and keep warm. Boil the pan liquids until they thicken and reduce to approximately 1 quart. Season with salt and pepper and pass through a fine-mesh strainer; discard the solids. (The ribs and sauce can be made a few days ahead and kept covered in the refrigerator. Reheat gently, basting frequently, on top of the stove or in a 350°F oven.)

Chef Tip: To serve, pour the sauce over the meat. Serve with a young brawny Médoc, such as a Pauillac or a Saint Julien.

Filet of Beef ◄ Colman Andrews
with marcillac wine sauce

Extra-virgin olive oil
2 medium carrots, peeled and chopped
2 stalks celery, chopped
1 small yellow onion, peeled and chopped
3 tablespoons cognac
1 cup red wine vinegar
3 cups marcillac, cahors, or other hearty red wine
3 cups veal stock
Cracked black pepper
4 6-ounce beef filets, each about 1½ inches thick
Coarse salt
2 tablespoons butter, cubed

HEAT 1 tablespoon oil in a heavy pot over medium heat, add carrots, celery, and onion, and sauté until browned, about 5 minutes. Add cognac and carefully ignite with a kitchen match; when flames die out, add vinegar, wine, veal stock, and 1 tablespoon pepper. Reduce heat to low and reduce sauce by three-quarters, about 1½ hours. Strain, discard solids, and set sauce aside.

SEASON filets to taste with salt. Heat 1 tablespoon oil in a heavy skillet over high heat until hot. Add filets and cook for 7 minutes on each side, then transfer to 4 plates. Reduce heat to medium, add sauce to skillet, whisk in butter, then spoon sauce over filets. **serves 4**

Chef Tip: Tie a piece of cotton kitchen twine snugly around the middle of each filet (or ask you butcher to do this for you) to keep the filets shapely as they cook; discard the twine before serving the filets.

Colman Andrews > Polka Dot Cheesecake

2 ounces unsweetened chocolate, chopped
2 pounds cream cheese
1 teaspoon vanilla extract
1/4 teaspoon almond extract
1 3/4 cups sugar
4 large eggs
1/3 cup graham cracker crumbs

ADJUST a rack to the lowest position in the oven and preheat oven to 350°F. Butter an 8×3-inch one-piece cheesecake pan all the way up to the rim and including the inside of the rim itself. You will also need a larger pan (for hot water) to place the cake pan in while baking. The larger pan must not be deeper than the cheesecake pan. Set aside.

IN the top of a small double boiler over hot water on low heat, melt the chocolate and set it aside. In the large bowl of an electric mixer, beat the cheese until it is completely smooth. During the beating, frequently scrape the sides and bottom of the bowl with a rubber spatula. When the cheese is smooth, beat in the vanilla and almond extracts and the sugar. Beat well and then add the eggs one at a time. After adding the eggs, do not beat any more than necessary to mix.

REMOVE the bowl from the mixer. Place one-third of the batter (2 cups)

in the small bowl of the electric mixer. Add the melted chocolate and beat until smooth.

SPRAY the buttered cake pan with nonstick spray, then pour in the light-colored mixture.

FIT a large (about 16 inches) pastry bag with a plain #6 (1/2 inch) tube. Fold down a deep cuff on the outside of the bag and twist the tube end of the bag to prevent the mixture from running out.

PLACE the chocolate mixture in the bag.

NOW, work at table height, not counter height (you will have better control at table height). Place the cake pan on the table. Unfold the cuff on the pastry bag. Untwist the tube end of the bag. Place the tip of the tube in the center of the top of the cake, inserting it 1/4 to 1/2 inch into the cake. Squeeze out enough of the chocolate mixture to form a perfectly round ball about 2 inches wide. There will now be a dark polka dot in the center of the cake.

THEN, using the same procedure, squeeze out 6 smaller balls around the rim. In order to space

the 6 balls evenly, place the first one at twelve o'clock (straight up), the next at six o'clock (straight down). Then, two on each side. Doing it this way, the chances are that the spacing will be quite even. The balls around the rim should be smaller than the one in the center, and they should not touch each other or the center ball. If you have some chocolate mixture left over, add it to the center ball; if you still have some left over, add a bit to each of the other balls.

THE top of the cake will not be smooth and level now, but it will level itself during baking. When baked, the polka dot in the center will be about 2 1/2 inches wide; the dots around the rim will be about 1 1/2 inches wide.

PLACE the cake pan into the larger pan. Place it in the oven and pour hot water into the larger pan, about 1 1/2 inches deep.

BAKE for 1 1/2 hours. The top of the cake will become golden-brown and it will feel dry to the touch. But the cake will still be soft inside (it will become firm when it has cooled and been refrigerated).

LIFT the cake pan out of the water

and place it on a cake rack. Cool the cake in the pan for 2½ hours. (Do not cool it in the refrigerator or the butter will harden and the cake will stick to the pan.)

COVER the pan with plastic wrap. Place a flat plate or small board upside down over the pan and turn the pan and the plate or board upside down. Carefully, remove the pan.

CAREFULLY and evenly sprinkle the graham cracker crumbs over the bottom of the cake. Gently place another flat plate or small board upside down over the cake and carefully invert again (without squashing the cake), leaving the cake right side up. Remove the plastic wrap. **makes one 8-inch cake**

Chef Tip: Refrigerate for several hours or overnight. To serve, dip a sharp knife in very hot water before making each cut (shake off the water but do not dry the blade). Make the first cut through the middle of one of smaller dots and the second cut (the one that will release the first portion) between two of the smaller dots.

Todd English > # Almond Amaretti Waffles

Peach Mascarpone Ice Cream

8 large egg yolks
3/4 cup sugar
1 1/2 cups milk
1 1/2 cups heavy cream
3 peaches, peeled, pitted and roughly chopped
1/2 teaspoon almond extract
1 teaspoon vanilla extract
1/2 teaspoon kosher salt
1 pound mascarpone
Reserve 1 1/2 cups fresh peaches (skins and pits removed—sliced in 8 to 10 wedges, wedges then cut in half)

PLACE the egg yolks and sugar in the bowl of a mixer fitted with a whisk and whip until stiff. Place the milk and heavy cream in a saucepan and bring to a boil over medium heat. Pour the hot milk mixture over the sugar, whisking all the while. Add the chopped peaches, extracts and salt and whisk to combine. Chill in an ice bath. Place the mascarpone in a large bowl and gradually add the sugar-milk mixture. Pour through a strainer and discard the solids. Transfer to an ice cream maker and freeze according to manufacturer's instructions. Fold in peach wedges, transfer to a bowl and freeze.

Almond Amaretti Waffles

1 3/4 cups flour
2 teaspoons double acting baking powder
1/2 teaspoon salt
1 tablespoon sugar
3 egg yolks
5 tablespoons melted butter
1 1/2 cups milk
1 tablespoon amaretto liqueur
1 teaspoon almond extract
3 egg whites, beaten to medium peaks

INTO a medium bowl, sift flour, baking powder, salt and sugar. Add liquid ingredients and mix just until they are incorporated—do not overmix. Carefully fold in egg whites. Pour recommended amount into waffle iron according to manufacturer's instructions.

Toasted Almond Brittle

1 cup sugar
1/2 cup light corn syrup
2 tablespoons water
3/4 cup almonds
3/4 ounces unsalted butter (1 1/2 tablespoons)
1/2 teaspoon vanilla extract
3/4 teaspoon baking soda

LAY a sheet of parchment onto a clean, flat, heat-resistant surface. In a small sauce pot fitted with a candy thermometer, combine sugar, corn syrup and water and cook to 295°F. Stir in almonds and butter. Remove from heat and stir in vanilla and baking soda. Quickly pour onto parchment and spread with an offset spatula. Let harden, then break into pieces.

Amaretti Cookie Crunch
3 to 4 amaretti cookies

LIGHTLY break cookies into ¼-inch chunks, careful not to pulverize.

Toasted Slivered Almonds
½ cup slivered almonds

SPREAD slivered almonds onto baking sheet or toaster oven tray and lightly toast to golden brown.

Amaretto Whipped Cream
1 cup heavy cream
1 tablespoon fine sugar
1 tablespoon amaretto liqueur
1 teaspoon almond extract

POUR cream into the bowl of a mixer with whipping attachment. Begin at medium speed. As it begins to thicken, add sugar and increase speed. Just as it begins to hold peaks (be careful not to overwhip), pour in liqueur and almond extract and whip just to incorporate.

TO ASSEMBLE: Take a warm amaretti waffle and top with peach ice cream, brittle, crunch, almonds and whipped cream. Serve immediately. **serves 4**

Chef Tip: Waffles are best eaten warm right off the griddle.

Crème Brûlée ◀ Ina Garten

1 extra-large egg
4 extra-large egg yolks
½ cup sugar, plus 1 tablespoon
   for each serving
3 cups heavy cream
1 teaspoon pure vanilla extract
1 tablespoon Grand Marnier

PREHEAT the oven to 300 degrees. In the bowl of an electric mixer fitted with the paddle attachment, mix the egg, egg yolks, and ½ cup of the sugar together on low speed until just combined. Meanwhile, scald the cream in a small saucepan until it's very hot to the touch but not boiled. With the mixer on low speed, slowly add the cream to the eggs. Add the vanilla and Grand Marnier and pour into 6- to 8-ounce ramekins until almost full.

PLACE the ramekins in a baking pan and carefully pour boiling water into the pan to come halfway up the sides of the ramekins. Bake for 35 to 40 minutes, until the custards are set when gently shaken. Remove the custards from the water bath, cool to room temperature, and refrigerate until firm.

TO SERVE, spread 1 tablespoon of sugar evenly on the top of each ramekin and heat with a kitchen blowtorch until the sugar caramelizes evenly. Allow to sit at room temperature for a minute until the caramelized sugar hardens. **serves 5 to 6**

Chef Tip: The custards can be made up to 3 days in advance; caramelize the tops before serving.

Casual **Cuisine**

Al Roker >

Q. Where did you learn to cook? Who inspired your interest in cooking?

A. I learned to cook from my mother. I used to watch her and always wanted to emulate what she did. I got my passion for cooking from my dad, who cooked and baked as a hobby.

Q. What is your first memory of cooking?

A. I remember around 6 years old making a hard-boiled egg sandwich. Two eggs, Wonder Bread, and Miracle Whip. Heaven.

Q. Since you have traveled across the globe, what is your favorite regional cuisine?

A. Whatever I'm eating at that moment.

Q. What meals do you make for your kids that they love?

A. I'm very lucky. My kids have eclectic tastes. From grilled cheese on whole wheat to sushi, they eat it all.

Q. What is your favorite gourmet meal to eat or prepare?

A. I don't do "gourmet." I like grilled, broiled, or roasted. Not a lot of sauces. Simple is better. If you use quality ingredients, the flavor shines through.

Q. What are your favorite spices for cooking?

A. Cumin, salt, pepper, and minced fresh garlic.

Q. What is your favorite recipe and where did you get it?

A. Toss up. Daniel Boulud's Braised Short Ribs with Yukon Gold Potato-Celery Root Puree and Judy Rogers' Roast Chicken and bread salad from the Zuni Cafe.

Q. What do you make when you are entertaining guests? Why?

A. I make either of these for guests. The short ribs are an all-day affair, but so very worth it when people take that first bite and sigh. The Roast Chicken is so simple, yet so satisfying.

Q. What is your favorite comfort food? What do you like to prepare when you are just cooking casually?

A. See above. But I also like making meat loaf, and believe or not, a good sloppy joe is hard to beat.

Q. What is the food that you should not eat but do?

A. I haven't had it in awhile, but scrapple is just the worst for you, and after eating it, you know you shouldn't have, but it is soooo good going down.

Q. Do you follow recipes or do you just like to experiment? Is cooking a creative process for you?

A. I like to do both. I use a recipe as a starting point and go from there. It's not only creative, but it's relaxing. I like looking in the pantry and the fridge and figuring out what to come up with for dinner. I'll stand in front of either for a few minutes and see what comes to me.

Q. Has your style of cooking changed over the years? If so, what influenced the change?

A. Going to Memphis in May. The BBQ festival really got me into barbecue and learning how to cook with a minimum of spice and ingredients and make the meat speak for itself.

Q. What do you eat for breakfast before the show?

A. A couple of spoonfuls of peanut butter and a slice of whole wheat toast.

Al's Chili ◄ Al Roker

2 pounds chuck steak, cubed
   in bite size pieces
1 pound hot Italian sausage,
   removed from casings
2 large onions, diced
12 cloves garlic, diced
1 tablespoon cumin
1 tablespoon paprika
1 tablespoon pure chili powder
1 32-ounce can crushed
   tomatoes
1 16-ounce can pinto beans
1 16-ounce can northern beans
1 16-ounce can dark red
   kidney beans

BROWN the beef and sausage in a large Dutch oven. Remove meat from pan and reserve. Drain off the fat, reserving about 2 tablespoons. Sauté the onions and garlic till translucent, about 7 to 8 minutes.

ADD the cumin, paprika, and chili powder. Then add the tomatoes and the meat into the Dutch oven.

Stir the whole pot, and simmer on the stove for about an hour and half. At that point, add the three cans of beans; simmer for another 30 minutes.

SERVE with dishes of chopped scallions, sour cream, and shredded cheddar cheese. A nice warm corn bread would be nice, as well. **serves 6 to 8**

Al Roker is the author of *Al Roker's Big Bad Book of Barbecue,* released in May 2002, which quickly became a summer blockbuster and a New York Times best-seller and has recently released a second cookbook *Al Roker's Hassle Free Holiday Cookbook* (Scribner).

Watermelon Gazpacho ◀ Tyler Florence

6 large tomatoes, pureed
8 ounces fresh watermelon
2 tablespoons red onion, minced
2 tablespoons fresh dill, minced
2 tablespoons red wine vinegar
1 serrano chili
¼ cup extra-virgin olive oil
1 cucumber, seeded and minced
¼ cup crumbled feta cheese
   Salt and freshly ground
      black pepper

IN a blender, pulse the tomatoes, chili, and watermelon until it is almost smooth. Add the red wine vinegar and olive oil and pulse until well combined. Fold in the onion, cucumber, and dill and season with salt and pepper.

CHILL for two hours and then season again before serving. Pour into shot glasses and garnish with dill and feta. Serve at room temperature. **serves 8**

Grilled Eggplant
with feta, mint and chili

Nigella Lawson

2 large eggplants, each cut thinly, lengthwise, into about 10 slices
4 tablespoons olive oil
8 to 9 ounces feta cheese
1 large red chili, finely chopped, seeded or not, depending on how much heat you want
Large bunch fresh mint, finely chopped, with some saved for sprinkling over at the end
Juice of 1 lemon
Black pepper

PREHEAT a grill, stovetop griddle or broiler to a high heat.

BRUSH both sides of the eggplant slices with the oil, and cook them for about 2 minutes each side until golden and tender.

CRUMBLE the feta into a bowl and stir in the chili, mint and lemon juice and grind in some black pepper. You don't need salt, as the feta is salty enough. Pile the end third of each warm eggplant slice with a heaping teaspoon of the feta mixture and roll each slice up as you go to form a soft, stuffed bundle.

PLACE seam-side down on a plate, and sprinkle with a little more mint. **makes 20 rolls**

Chef Tip: Grill the eggplant slices well in advance so that all you need to do when you want to eat is add the cheese and chili and do a quick, easy, last-minute roll up before serving.

Grilled Vegetable Antipasto *with herbed chèvre and crostini*

> **S**ara **F**oster

Safflower oil or canola oil, for oiling the grill
½ cup olive oil
¼ cup balsamic vinegar
5 fresh basil leaves, cut into thin strips (chiffonade)
2 zucchini, cut into ½-inch slices lengthwise
2 yellow squash, cut into ½-inch slices lengthwise
1 red onion, cut into ½-inch-thick round slices
2 red bell peppers, cored, seeded and cut into 2-inch strips
7 scallions, trimmed
Salt and freshly ground black pepper to taste
¼ cup sun-dried tomatoes
2 large ripe tomatoes cut into ½-inch slices
1 recipe Herbed Chèvre
1 recipe Herbed Balsamic Vinaigrette
Fresh parsley and fresh basil leaves for garnish, optional
Crostini (recipe follows)

BRUSH the grill grates lightly with safflower oil. Prepare a hot fire on a gas or charcoal grill. Whisk together olive oil, vinegar and basil in a small bowl until well blended. Brush the zucchini, yellow squash, onion, red bell peppers and scallions with the olive oil mixture. Place the vegetables on the hot grill and cook 3 to 4 minutes per side until crisp-tender. Season with salt and pepper.

SOAK sun-dried tomatoes in 1 cup hot water, covered, about 5 minutes or until softened. Drain and set aside. (Note: Eliminate this step if you are using sun-dried tomatoes packed in oil.)

ARRANGE the grilled vegetables, sun-dried tomatoes and sliced tomatoes on individual plates or a serving platter. Add a slice of chèvre on the side of the vegetables. Drizzle vegetables with vinaigrette and drizzle a little more vinaigrette around the plate. Garnish with the parsley and basil. Season with additional salt and pepper if desired and serve with Crostini. serves 8

Herbed Chèvre
¼ cup fresh parsley, chopped, or mixed fresh herbs such as thyme, rosemary and dill
1 tablespoon freshly ground black pepper
1 8-ounce mild creamy chèvre log

MIX the parsley and pepper together on a plate. Roll the chèvre log in the mixture, pressing lightly so the seasonings adhere. Wrap in plastic wrap and chill 1 to 2 hours. Remove log from the refrigerator and unwrap. Cut into 1-inch slices with string, dental floss or wire. Keep refrigerated until ready to serve.

Herbed Balsamic Vinaigrette
⅓ cup balsamic vinegar
Juice of 1 lemon
2 tablespoons mixed chopped fresh basil, parsley and thyme
1 teaspoon freshly ground black pepper
¼ cup extra-virgin olive oil
⅓ cup canola or safflower oil

COMBINE the vinegar, lemon juice, herbs, and pepper in a small bowl and stir to mix. Slowly add the olive oil and canola oil and whisk until all the oil is incorporated. Refrigerate in an airtight container until ready to use or up to 1 week. **makes about 1 cup vinaigrette**

Crostini
1 baguette, cut into ¼-inch slices on the diagonal
¼ cup olive oil
Freshly ground pepper to taste

PREHEAT oven to 400°F. Place baguette slices in one layer on a baking sheet. Brush with olive oil, sprinkle with pepper and bake 10 to 15 minutes, until golden brown. Remove from oven and set aside to cool.

Chef Tip; You can also pile the grilled vegetables onto crusty French bread that's been slathered with creamy chèvre. The vegetables can be grilled up to 1 hour in advance; assemble just before serving.

Tom Colicchio > Roasted Carrots

30 baby carrots (3 to 4 inches long)
2 tablespoons peanut oil
  Kosher salt and freshly
  ground black pepper
2 tablespoons unsalted butter
2 sprigs of rosemary

PEEL the carrots, then trim them, leaving an inch or so of the green top.

HEAT a large skillet over medium heat. Add the oil, then the carrots. Salt and pepper them.

COOK, rolling the carrots so they color on all sides, until they are golden, about 5 minutes. Add the butter and rosemary and continue cooking until the carrots are tender, about 5 minutes more. Drain the carrots on paper towels before serving. serves 6

Chef Tip: We use baby carrots for this dish, but it would work equally well with mature carrots, cut to size. We recommend tasting a tip of the raw carrot and using those that have a bright, sweet flavor—these have the highest sugar levels and will caramelize nicely as they cook.

Black-Eyed Pea Rice Pilaf

< Tanya Holland

1 cup black-eyed peas, rinsed
   and soaked overnight
1½ teaspoons coarse salt
½ pound snow peas, trimmed
1 tablespoon unsalted butter
1 tablespoon vegetable or olive oil
1 onion, minced
2 cloves garlic, minced
1½ cups uncooked basmati rice
3 cups vegetable stock
¼ teaspoon freshly ground
   white pepper
½ pound fresh, shelled English
   peas or frozen green peas
2 tablespoons chopped parsley
1 tablespoon lemon zest
   Fresh pea shoots, for garnish
   (optional)

IN a small pot, cover black-eyed peas with water. Bring to a boil, skimming off any impurities, and cook 20 minutes, or until soft but not mushy. Bring the water to a boil, add 1 teaspoon salt, and cook snow peas 1 minute, or until they turn a vibrant green but are still crunchy. Drain snow peas and cover with cold water, strain, and set aside. Cut the snow peas into julienned strips.

IN a large skillet over medium heat, add butter and oil; cook onion and garlic until soft, about 5 minutes.

ADD rice and cook an additional 5 minutes. Add stock, remaining ½ teaspoon salt, and white pepper; bring to a boil, and then reduce to a simmer. Continue to cook, covered, ½ hour. Add reserved snow peas, English peas, black-eyed peas, parsley, and zest. Mix well and adjust seasonings to taste. Garnish with pea shoots if desired. serves 6

Chef Tip: Soaking beans overnight will reduce the cooking time. Lemon zest and juice can brighten the taste of many savory foods; the acidity can help balance the flavor of a dish.

Marinated Butternut Squash *(scapece di zucca)* < **M**ario **B**atali

2   medium butternut squash,
    seeded and cut into
    1-inch slices
    Salt and pepper
4   tablespoons plus
    4 tablespoons extra-virgin
    olive oil
¼   cup red wine vinegar
½   medium red onion, sliced
    paper thin
½   teaspoon red chile flakes
1   tablespoon dried oregano
1   clove garlic, sliced paper-thin
¼   cup fresh mint leaves

PREHEAT oven to 450°F. Season the squash with salt and pepper, drizzle with 4 tablespoons olive oil, and place in a single layer on 1 or 2 cookie sheets. Bake in the oven until just tender, about 18 to 20 minutes. Meanwhile, stir together the remaining oil, vinegar, onion, chile flakes, oregano, and garlic and season with salt and pepper.

REMOVE the squash from the oven and pour the marinade over. Allow to cool for 20 minutes in the marinade, sprinkle with fresh mint leaves, and serve. This dish can be made earlier in the day but should not be refrigerated. **serves 8**

Liz Weiss > Corny Salmon Cakes

2 6-ounce cans boneless,
skinless pink salmon, drained
and finely flaked
1 cup dried bread crumbs, divided
³/₄ cup preshredded reduced-fat
Cheddar cheese
³/₄ cup frozen corn kernels, thawed
¹/₃ cup light canola mayonnaise
2 tablespoons ketchup
1 large egg, beaten
1 tablespoon canola oil

COMBINE the salmon, ¹/₂ cup bread crumbs, cheese, corn, mayonnaise, ketchup, and egg in a bowl and mix until well blended. Shape the mixture into 8 patties and coat with the remaining ¹/₂ cup bread crumbs. Heat half the oil in a large nonstick skillet over medium heat. Cook the patties until golden brown,

5 minutes. Add the remaining oil to the skillet, flip the patties, and cook an additional 4 to 5 minutes.
serves 4

Chef Tip: For a colorful variation and some extra nutrition, replace the corn with one large carrot, peeled and shredded.

Braised Red Snapper Tyler Florence

with grandma-style zucchini, peppers & black olives

3 red bell peppers
Extra-virgin olive oil
Sea salt and freshly ground
   black pepper
15 baby new potatoes, halved
3 zucchini, cut in ½-inch-
   thick circles
½ cup whole kalamata olives
3 garlic cloves, sliced
2 fresh thyme sprigs
6 fresh tarragon leaves
½ lemon, sliced paper-thin
2 cups chicken stock
1 cup dry white wine, such as
   Sauvignon Blanc
Juice of 1 lemon
2 center-cut red snapper fillets,
   about 8 ounces each, skin
   on, halved on the diagonal

PREHEAT the broiler. Pull out the cores of the red peppers; then halve them lengthwise and remove the ribs and seeds. Toss the peppers with a little olive oil, salt, and pepper. Place them on a cookie sheet, skin sides up, and broil for 10 minutes, until really charred and blistered. Put the peppers into a bowl, cover with plastic wrap, and steam for about 10 minutes to loosen the skins.

PEEL the peppers and cut them into big strips.

HEAT a 2-count of oil in a wide pot. Add the roasted peppers, potatoes, zucchini, olives, garlic, thyme, tarragon, and lemon slices. Sauté everything together for a few minutes over medium heat to coat in the oil and soften; season with salt and pepper. Add the chicken stock, wine, and lemon juice. Bring to a boil, then reduce the heat, and let it slowly simmer down for 30 minutes while you prepare the fish.

RUB a little olive oil and salt and pepper on the fish fillets. Add a 2-count drizzle of olive oil to a skillet and place over medium heat. When the pan is nice and hot, sear the fish, skin side down. Gently press on the fish with a spatula to crisp up the skin. Carefully transfer the fish to the pot of vegetables, skin side up. Turn the heat down to low, cover, and simmer for 5 minutes. Keep an eye on it; don't let the liquid boil or cook the fish too long or it will fall apart. Serve the fish and vegetables in wide, shallow bowls with a ladle of broth and a drizzle of olive oil.
serves 2

Chef Tip: "Grandma-style" means the vegetables are cooked like a stew in a pot until they're soft and delicious. This is one of the classic recipes I pull out in a pinch, and it's always welcomed.

Shrimp Teriyaki Noodles ◄ Liz Weiss

8 ounces medium curly egg noodles (about 4 cups)
1 16-ounce bag frozen broccoli florets, thawed
1 16-ounce bag frozen precooked small or medium shrimp, thawed
1 tablespoon peanut oil
⅓ cup reduced-sodium (lite) teriyaki sauce
⅓ cup water
1 tablespoon reduced-sodium (lite) soy sauce
2 teaspoons cornstarch
Chopped peanuts (optional)

BRING a big saucepan of water to a boil. Add the noodles and cook according to package directions. A few minutes before the noodles are done, stir in the broccoli. Bring the water back to a boil and cook until the pasta and broccoli are cooked to your liking. Drain and set aside. Return the saucepan to the stove and heat the oil over medium-high heat. Add the shrimp and sauté 1 to 2 minutes. Meanwhile, whisk together the teriyaki sauce, water, soy sauce, and cornstarch. Once the shrimp are hot, add the well-blended teriyaki mixture to the pan and stir for a minute or two until the sauce thickens. Add the broccoli and pasta back to the pan, mix everything together, and heat through. For added flavor and crunch, top with chopped peanuts. **serves 5**

Chef Tip: Use canola oil instead of peanut oil if someone in your family has a peanut allergy.

Nigella Lawson > Cold Roast Beef
with lemon salad

5½ pounds (or there abouts) top loin or tenderloin if you're feeling extravagant (or whatever cut of beef you prefer)
5 lemons
1 teaspoon Maldon or other sea salt
3 fresh red chilies, seeded and finely chopped
5 tablespoons fresh parsley, chopped
5 tablespoons extra-virgin olive oil
1 head frisée (curly endive) lettuce
2 heads radicchio
4 romaine lettuce hearts
Approximately 3-ounce block Parmesan

PREHEAT the oven to 425°F. For rare beef, cook for 12 minutes per pound; it will continue cooking as it cools so be prepared to take it out of the oven when it still looks underdone to you.

THIS should give you divinely ruby-rare roast beef; obviously, though, cook for longer if you want it less red. Anyway, set aside till cool. If, however, you're going to eat the roast beef rare and hot, then just stick it in the hottest oven you can for 15 minutes and then turn the oven down to 350°F and cook it for 15 minutes per pound plus 15 minutes at the end. I'm hesitant about making this all sound too exact, because ovens vary enormously and the length of time it takes to roast rare roast beef in one oven can leave it either leathery and overcooked or still cold in the middle in another. Perhaps I exaggerate, but not by much. Probably the best advice is to say to go slowly and test often, though not stabbing (you don't want to lose all of the glorious red juices) but by pressing: when the beef's rare it will feel soft and eiderdown-bouncy to the touch; when medium rare it will feel springy; when well cooked it will have pretty much no bounce left in it. Of course, you can pierce with a knife to make really sure, but just try to leave that to the end, rather than puncture repeatedly throughout its cooking.

TO make the salad, cut the tops and bottoms off the lemons. Sit them upright on a board on one end, and cut away the zest and pith from top to bottom with a sharp knife till only the juicy lemon remains. Now slice into rounds then chop each round into about four, and place on a large plate or shallow bowl. Sprinkle the salt over them then scatter with the chopped chilies and parsley and pour over the oil. Leave to steep while you carve the beef and get on with the rest of the salad. Which simply means, tear the frisée, radicchio and romaine hearts into rough pieces and mix together in a large bowl. Shave in most of the Parmesan with a vegetable peeler and pour in most of the lemon chunks, and all their oily juices. Mix together thoroughly with your fingers then decant onto a couple of large, flat serving plates (I so much prefer salad on plates than in bowls), adding any more oil (or indeed lemon juice) if you think the dressing needs thus augmenting, then add the remaining lemon chunks and shave in a final few slithering curls of Parmesan.
serves 10

What a Back
with glaze

Karen Brooks & Diane Morgan

3 racks pork baby back ribs
  (about 1½ pounds each)
3 cups Hidden Pleasures Hoisin-
  Ginger Glaze (recipe follows)
3 cups hickory or apple wood chips
  Disposable foil pan
  Vegetable oil for brushing

PLACE the ribs flat in a nonreactive roasting pan, or "roll" the racks and fit them into a 1½-gallon resealable plastic bag. Set aside ½ cup of the glaze. Pour the remaining glaze over the ribs, rubbing it onto both sides like a good back massage. (Get one yourself while the ribs are relaxing in the glaze. Beg, plead, or threaten to withhold ribs.) Cover the pan with plastic wrap or tightly seal the bag. Refrigerate 6 to 8 hours to blend the flavors.

SOAK the wood chips in cold water to cover for 1 hour. Set up the grill for indirect cooking. Prepare a medium fire in a charcoal grill or preheat one side of a gas or electric grill on medium. Drain the chips and sprinkle half of them over the coals, or place half in the grill's smoker box. Place a disposable foil pan under the grate to catch drippings.

BRUSH the grill grate with vegetable oil. Arrange the ribs, meaty-side down, on the side of the grill without hot coals. Cover the grill and smoke-cook the ribs 45 minutes. Turn the ribs and add the remaining wood chips. Cover and grill another 45 minutes. Brush the ribs with half of the reserved glaze. Using long-handled tongs, slide the ribs onto the grate directly over the hot coals. Grill, uncovered, 5 minutes. Turn the ribs over, baste again, and grill another 5 minutes. Cut between the bones, slicing the racks into individual ribs. Serve immediately. **serves 4 to 6**

Chef Tip: Leave the smoked-all-day spareribs to the dudes. Pork baby backs are sweet and tender and good to go in under two hours on the grill. Use the marinating time to primp and polish.

Hidden Pleasures
Hoisin-Ginger Glaze
  1 cup hoisin sauce
  ½ cup plum sauce
  ½ low-sodium soy sauce
  ¼ Asian sesame oil
  2 tablespoons minced
    fresh ginger
1½ tablespoons minced garlic
  1 teaspoon freshly
    ground pepper
  ¼ cup honey

IN a medium bowl combine all ingredients. Stir thoroughly to blend. Use immediately, or cover and refrigerate up to 1 month. **makes about 3 cups**

Kansas City Sweet-and-Smoky Ribs

Steven Raichlen

4 racks of spareribs (4 to 6 pounds total)
6 cups apple cider, plus additional for spraying the ribs
4 whole lemons (optional), halved
⅔ cup Basic Barbecue Rub or your favorite commercial brand
3 cups of your favorite homemade barbecue sauce or your favorite commercial brand

For Barbecue Rub:
2 tablespoons brown sugar
2 tablespoons sweet paprika
4 teaspoons salt
2 teaspoons garlic powder
2 teaspoons black pepper
1 teaspoon ground cumin

For Citrus Barbecue Sauce:
2 cups ketchup
½ cup brown sugar
2 teaspoons grated fresh lemon zest (the oil rich outer rind)
⅓ cup fresh lemon juice, or to taste
3 tablespoons molasses
1 tablespoon Worcestershire sauce
1 tablespoon Dijon mustard
2 teaspoons liquid smoke
1 teaspoon garlic powder
½ teaspoon freshly ground black pepper

TRIM each rack of ribs or have your butcher do this for you.

PLACE the ribs in a large nonreactive roasting pan. Pour the cider over the ribs. Squeeze the juice from the lemons over the ribs, catching the seeds with your fingers. Turn the ribs a couple of times to coat all over with marinade. If desired, let the ribs marinate in the refrigerator, covered, for 4 to 6 hours, turning several times.

DRAIN the ribs and blot dry with paper towels. Sprinkle ½ cup of the rub on both sides of the ribs, patting it onto the meat with your fingers. Let the ribs stand in the refrigerator, covered, for 1 to 2 hours.

SET up the grill for indirect grilling and preheat to medium. If using a charcoal grill, place a large drip pan in the center. If using a gas grill, place all the wood chips in the smoker box or in a smoker pouch and preheat to high until you see smoke, then reduce the heat to medium.

WHEN ready to cook, if using charcoal, toss 1 cup of wood chips on the coals. Place the ribs in the center of the hot grate, away from the heat. Cover the grill and cook the ribs for 2 to 3 hours. After 30 minutes, spray the ribs with apple cider and continue to spray every half hour until ready to brush with the sauce. If using a charcoal grill, you'll need to add 12 fresh coals and ½ cup wood chips per side after each hour.

LIGHTLY brush the ribs with 1 cup of the sauce 20 minutes before the ribs are done. When the ribs are fully cooked, the meat will have shrunk back from the bones about ¼ inch, and the meat will be tender enough to tear apart with your fingers. But don't overcook; the ribs should have some chew to them. If the ribs start to dry out, wrap them in aluminum foil for the last hour of cooking.

TRANSFER the ribs to plates or a platter. Sprinkle the ribs with the remaining rub and lightly brush again with barbecue sauce. Let the ribs rest for a few minutes, then serve with the remaining barbecue sauce on the side. serves 6 to 8

For Barbecue Rub:
COMBINE the ingredients in a mixing bowl and stir to mix. Store the rub in an airtight jar away from heat or light; it will keep for at least 6 months.

For Citrus Barbecue Sauce:
COMBINE the ingredients in a saucepan and whisk to mix. Gradually bring the sauce to a simmer over medium heat and simmer until thick and flavorful, 8 to 10 minutes. Transfer to a bowl or clean jars and let cool to room temperature. Refrigerate until serving.

Steven Raichlen > The One and Only
Beer-Can Chicken

1 can (12 ounces) beer
1 chicken (3¹/₂ to 4 pounds)
2 tablespoons Basic Barbecue
   Rub (see page 107) or your
   favorite commercial rub

POP the tab off the beer can. Using a church key-style can opener, make a few more holes in the top of the can. Pour out half the beer into the soaking water of the wood chips. Set the can of beer aside.

SET up the grill for indirect grilling and preheat to medium. If using a charcoal grill, place a large drip pan in the center. If using a gas grill, place all the wood chips or chunks in the smoker box or in a smoker pouch and preheat on high until you see smoke, then reduce the heat to medium.

REMOVE the packet of giblets from the body cavity of the chicken and set aside for another use. Remove and discard the fat just inside the body and neck cavities. Rinse the chicken, inside and out, under cold running water and then drain and blot dry, inside and out, with paper towels. Sprinkle 2 teaspoons of the rub inside the body and neck cavities of the chicken. Rub the bird all over on the outside with 2 teaspoons of the rub. If you have the patience, you can put some of the rub under the skin.

SPOON the remaining 2 teaspoons of rub through the holes into the beer in the can. Don't worry if it foams up: This is normal. Insert the beer can into the body cavity of the chicken and spread out the legs to form a sort of tripod. Tuck the wing tips behind the chicken's back.

WHEN ready to cook, if using a charcoal grill, toss all the wood chips on the coals. Stand the chicken up in the center of the hot grate, over the drip pan and away from the heat. Cover the grill and cook the chicken until the skin is a dark golden brown and very crisp and the meat is cooked through (about 180°F on an instant-read meat thermometer inserted in the thigh), 1¹/₄ to 1¹/₂ hours. If using a charcoal grill, you'll need to add 12 fresh coals per side after 1 hour.

USING tongs, carefully transfer the chicken in its upright position on the beer can to a platter and present it to your guests. Let rest 5 minutes, then carefully remove the chicken from the beer can. Take care not to spill the hot beer or otherwise burn yourself. (Normally I discard the beer, but some people like to save it for making barbecue sauce.) Quarter or carve the chicken and serve. **serves 2 to 4**

Spit-Roasted Lamb
with berber spices
Steven **R**aichlen

For the spice paste:
- 1 small onion, coarsely chopped
- 1 piece (2 inches) fresh ginger, peeled and coarsely chopped
- 2 cloves garlic, coarsely chopped
- 1 to 2 jalapeño peppers, seeded and coarsely chopped (for a hotter spice paste, leave the seeds in)
- 1/4 cup sweet paprika
- 1 tablespoon coarse salt (kosher or sea), or more to taste
- 2 teaspoons cracked black peppercorns
- 2 teaspoons ground coriander
- 1 teaspoon ground cumin
- 1/2 teaspoon ground cardamom
- 1/2 teaspoon ground cinnamon
- 1/2 teaspoon ground fenugreek (optional)
- 1/4 teaspoon ground allspice
- 1/8 teaspoon ground cloves
- 1/3 cup olive oil
- 3 tablespoons fresh lemon juice or more to taste

- 1 bone-in leg of lamb (4 to 5 pounds)
- 2 tablespoons (1/4 stick) unsalted butter (optional), melted
- Butcher's string

MAKE the spice paste: Place the onion, ginger, garlic, and jalapeño(s) in a food processor and finely chop, running the machine in short bursts. Add the paprika, salt, cracked pepper, coriander, cumin, cardamom, cinnamon, fenugreek, if using, allspice, and cloves and process until smooth. Gradually add the olive oil and lemon juice. Taste for seasoning, adding more salt and/or lemon juice as necessary; the mixture should be highly seasoned.

USING the tip of a paring knife, make small slits on all sides of the roast about 1½ inches apart. Using the tip of your index finger, widen the holes slightly. Place a tiny spoonful of spice paste in each slit, forcing it in with your finger. Spread the remaining spice paste over the roast. Tie the lamb into a tight cylinder with butcher's string. You can cook the lamb right away, but it will have even more flavor if you let it marinate in the refrigerator, covered, for 4 to 6 hours.

WHEN ready to cook, place the drip pan in the bottom of the rotisserie. Skewer the lamb lengthwise on the rotisserie spit. Attach the spit to the rotisserie and turn on the motor. If your rotisserie has a temperature control, set it to 400°F. Cook the roast until it is dark brown on all sides and cooked to taste, 1¼ to 1½ hours for medium-rare, about 1¾ hours for medium (most Moroccans prefer their lamb medium to well-done). Use an instant-read meat thermometer to test for doneness; don't let the thermometer touch the spit or a bone. Medium-rare lamb will have an internal temperature of about 145°F; medium lamb will be about 160°F.

TRANSFER the roast to a platter or cutting board, remove the spit, and let the meat rest for 5 minutes. Cut off and discard the string. Brush the lamb with butter, if desired (this may seem like gilding the lily, but it makes a luscious dish even richer). Thinly slice the lamb off the bone across the grain and serve at once. **serves 6 to 8**

Chef Tip: Fenugreek (literally "Greek hay") is a small rectangular seed with an earthy, pleasantly bitter flavor. Look for it at Indian markets, where it goes by the name methi.

Chile-Rubbed Brisket ◄ Ivy Stark

6 ancho chiles, seeded and stemmed
4 chiles de arbol, seeded and stemmed
1½ cups dry red wine
¼ cup rice vinegar
6 cloves garlic
2 teaspoons cumin, toasted and freshly ground
2 teaspoons dried oregano leaves
½ teaspoon canela (Mexican cinnamon)
1 piece (2½ to 3 pounds) center-cut beef brisket, surface fat trimmed
4 medium onions, thinly sliced

TOAST the chiles lightly in a dry sauté pan until they just begin to lighten in color. Remove to a pot with about 1 quart of water and bring to a boil. Remove from heat and let chiles stand in hot water until soft, about 15 minutes.

REMOVE the chiles from the water and puree in a blender with the wine, vinegar, garlic, cumin, oregano and canela until smooth.

SEASON meat on both sides with salt and pepper. Place in a roasting pan and cover with chile mixture and onions. Seal pan tightly with aluminum foil and cover. Roast at 350°F for about 4 hours until brisket is very tender. serves 6

Nigella Lawson > Chocolate Cherry Trifle

- 2 chocolate pound cakes
  (each approximately
  12 ounces)
- 1/2 cup black cherry jam
- 1/2 cup cherry brandy
- 2 cups bottled or canned sour
  cherries, drained

Custard
- 4 ounces bittersweet chocolate,
  minimum 70% cocoa solids
- 1 1/3 cups plus 1 tablespoon milk
- 1 1/2 cups plus 1 tablespoon
  heavy cream
- 8 egg yolks
- 1/2 cup plus 1 tablespoon
  superfine sugar
- 1/3 cup unsweetened cocoa

Topping
- 3 cups heavy cream
- 1 ounce bittersweet chocolate,
  as before

SLICE the chocolate loaves or cake and make jam sandwiches with the cherry jam. Layer into the bottom of a large trifle bowl. Pour over the cherry brandy so that the cake soaks it up, and then tip in the drained cherries. Cover with plastic wrap and leave to macerate while you make the custard.

CHOP up the chocolate and melt it; I do this on low to medium heat in the microwave, checking after 2 minutes, though it will probably need 4. Or you can stick the bowl over a pan of gently simmering water. Once the chocolate's melted, leave to one side while you get on with the custard proper.

WARM the milk and cream in a saucepan, and whisk the yolks, sugar and cocoa in a large bowl. Pour the warm milk and cream into the bowl, whisking it into the yolks and sugar mixture. Stir in the melted chocolate, scraping the sides well with a rubber spatula to get all of it in, and pour the custard back into the rinsed saucepan.

COOK over a medium heat until the custard thickens, stirring all the time. Make sure it doesn't boil, as it will split and curdle. Keep a sink full of cold water so that if you get scared you can plunge the custard

pan into the cold water and whisk like mad, which will avert possible crisis. The custard will get darker as it cooks and the flecks of chocolate will melt once the custard has thickened. And you do need this thick, so don't panic so much that you stop cooking while it's still runny. Admittedly, it carries on thickening as it cools and then when it's chilling in the fridge. Once it's ready, pour into a bowl to cool and cover the top of the custard with plastic wrap to stop it forming a skin. When the custard is cold, pour and scrape it over the chocolate cake layer in the trifle bowl, and leave in the fridge to set, covered in plastic wrap, overnight.

DECORATE when you are ready; whip the cream for the topping softly and spread it gently over the layer of custard. Grate the chocolate over the top. Let people fall upon it with greed and gratitude. They will go home happy. **serves 16**

Honey Almond Cake ◄ Ivy Stark

1 cup hot water
1 cup honey
1 pinch salt
¼ cup sugar
2 teaspoons baking soda
1 teaspoon baking powder
¼ cup dark rum (or water)
1 teaspoon fennel seed, ground
½ teaspoon nutmeg
1 teaspoon canela (Mexican cinnamon), ground
1 tablespoon crystallized ginger, chopped
2 cups rye flour
1½ cups unbleached all-purpose flour
1 teaspoon grated orange zest
1 cup golden raisins
1 cup almonds, toasted lightly and chopped
6 Granny Smith apples
1 Mexican vanilla bean, split and scraped
¼ cup brown sugar
¼ pound butter

PREHEAT oven to 400°F. Grease 9×5 inch loaf pan, and line bottom with greased parchment paper.

IN a large bowl, pour the hot water over the honey, and stir to thin consistency. Add the salt, sugar, baking soda, and baking powder; stir to dissolve. Add the rum, spices, and crystallized ginger; stir until combined thoroughly. Add rye flour slowly and combine well; then add all-purpose flour slowly, then add the orange rind, raisins, and almonds, stirring to combine thoroughly.

TRANSFER to the prepared pan and bake 10 minutes. Reduce the oven temperature to 350°F and bake until golden brown, about 1 hour 20 minutes. Test for doneness with a skewer inserted in the center of the cake; when it comes out clean and dry, it is done.

COOL the cake on a rack.

PEEL and quarter apples, place in a large saucepan with the vanilla bean, brown sugar, and butter. Simmer over low heat until apples are soft. Serve warm over the cake slices. **makes one 9×5-inch cake**

Raspberry-Almond Dream Cream

Sara **C**orpening **W**hiteford
& Mary **C**orpening **B**arber

1¼ teaspoons unflavored gelatin
1 cup milk
1 cup heavy cream
½ vanilla bean (3-inch piece) or
   ¼ teaspoon vanilla extract
⅓ cup sugar
   Pinch of kosher salt
¼ teaspoon almond extract
¾ cup fresh raspberries
   Fresh mint sprigs for garnishing

WHISK together the gelatin and milk in a medium bowl. Set aside until the gelatin softens, about 5 minutes.

COMBINE the cream, vanilla bean or extract, sugar, and kosher salt in a small saucepan over medium-high heat. Bring just to a boil, whisking frequently. Remove the pan from the heat. If using a vanilla bean, transfer the softened bean to a cutting board and let cool slightly. Meanwhile, add the hot cream mixture to the softened gelatin mixture, then add the almond extract and whisk until incorporated. Using a sharp knife, split the vanilla bean lengthwise, scrape out the small seeds, and add to the cream mixture. Discard the pod. Whisk until the mixture is smooth and the gelatin is dissolved.

STRAIN the mixture into a bowl and pour about ½ cup into each of 4 martini glasses, juice cups, or ramekins. Drop 6 to 8 raspberries into each glass. Let cool slightly, cover with plastic wrap, and refrigerate until set, about 2½ hours. (When set, they should still be slightly loose in the center.) Garnish with mint sprigs just before serving. **serves 4**

Chef Tip: These desserts can be made one day in advance. Keep refrigerated until ready to serve. Inspired by Italian panna cotta, this foolproof recipe is even easier when it comes to entertaining because there is no fussy unmolding.

Maple-Glazed Bananas ◄ Steven Raichlen

4 bananas (see Chef Tip)
3 tablespoons maple syrup
6 to 8 tablespoons dark brown
   sugar or confectioners' sugar
   Ground cinnamon
6 tablespoons Hot Fudge Sauce
   (optional; recipe follows)
6 tablespoons Cinnamon
   Caramel Sauce (optional;
   recipe follows)
   Vanilla ice cream (optional),
   for serving

PLACE the bananas on a work surface and cut each in half lengthwise (leave the skins on). Brush the cut sides with the maple syrup and generously sprinkle brown sugar over them. Lightly dust the cut sides of the bananas with cinnamon.

COOK the bananas on a grill until the cut side is caramelized to a dark golden brown and the fruit starts to pull away from the peel.

TRANSFER the grilled banana halves still in their skins to a platter or plates and place a scoop of vanilla ice cream alongside, if desired. Drizzle Hot Fudge Sauce and/or Cinnamon Caramel Sauce over all, if desired. **serves 4**

Chef Tip: The best bananas for grilling will be just shy of ripe and have firm yellow skins but won't have any of the tiny brown "sugar" spots that indicate the bananas are completely ripe.

Hot Fudge Sauce
$1/4$ cup unsweetened cocoa powder
$1/2$ cup sugar
$1/2$ cup heavy (whipping) cream
$1/4$ cup light corn syrup
3 ounces unsweetened chocolate,
   coarsely chopped
2 tablespoons ($1/4$ stick)
   unsalted butter
1 teaspoon vanilla extract
   A pinch salt

PLACE the cocoa powder and sugar in the top of a double boiler or in a metal mixing bowl over a saucepan of briskly simmering water. Whisk until well mixed. Add the cream and corn syrup and whisk to mix. Cook the cream mixture over briskly simmering water until thick and creamy, 3 to 5 minutes, whisking steadily.

ADD the chocolate, butter, vanilla, and salt, stir to mix, and cook until the chocolate and butter are melted and the sauce is smooth and creamy, 2 to 3 minutes. Keep the sauce warm until ready to serve. The sauce can be refrigerated, covered, for several weeks. Let it come to room temperature, then reheat it in a double boiler before serving. **makes 1$1/2$ cups**

Cinnamon Caramel Sauce
$3/4$ cup sugar
3 tablespoons hot water
$2/3$ cup heavy (whipping) cream
$1/2$ teaspoon ground cinnamon

PLACE the sugar and hot water in a heavy saucepan and gently stir with a wooden spoon to mix. Cover the saucepan, place it over high heat, and bring to a boil. Let the sugar mixture boil until clear, about 1 minute. Using a natural bristle pastry brush dipped in cold water, wash any sugar crystals down from the side of the saucepan.

UNCOVER the saucepan and let the sugar mixture cook until thick and deep golden brown, 5 to 8 minutes. You can gently shake the pan so the sugar cooks evenly, but don't stir it.

REMOVE the saucepan from the heat and add the cream and cinnamon. Stand back—it will bubble and hiss. Return the saucepan to the heat and let the sauce simmer until it is thick and creamy, about 3 minutes, stirring to mix with a wooden spoon. Let the caramel sauce cool to room temperature before serving. The sauce can be refrigerated, covered, for several weeks. Let it return to room temperature before serving. **makes 1$1/2$ cups**

Aaron **S**anchez > Pi-A Asada
(Broiled Pineapple)

1 large pineapple
½ cup sugar
Finely grated zest of 1 lime
1 teaspoon ground cinnamon,
preferably Mexican canela
½ cup (1 stick) unsalted butter,
melted

PREHEAT the broiler. Using a large sharp knife, cut off the leaves of the pineapple. Slice off the bottom to stabilize the base and stand the pineapple up. Cut off the rind from top to bottom, removing as much of the eyes as possible. Turn the pineapple on its side and slice crosswise into ½-inch-thick rounds. Cut the core out of each slice with a paring knife. Arrange the pineapple rings on a sheet pan lined with aluminum foil. In a small bowl, toss together the sugar, lime zest, and cinnamon. Brush the pineapple with the melted butter and sprinkle with the sugar mixture. Broil until caramelized and bubbly, about 2 to 4 minutes. **serves 4 to 6 (2 to 4 rings per serving)**

Decaf Coffee Granita ◄ **S**uzanne **S**omers

2 cups boiling water
¼ cup strong decaf coffee
2 cups heavy cream
3 tablespoons SomerSweet
(or ¾ cup sugar)
1 recipe Perfectly Whipped Cream

For Perfectly Whipped Cream:
2 cups whipping cream
1 teaspoon vanilla
2 teaspoons SomerSweet (or
2 tablespoons powdered
sugar)

WHISK together boiling water and decaf coffee in a large mixing bowl. Stir in cream and SomerSweet. Cool to room temperature. Place in a glass 9×9 inch baking dish and place in the freezer. As soon as the ice starts to appear on the edges (about three hours), stir the mixture with a fork. Continue to stir and break up ice every hour until mixture is slushy. Use a fork to flake the granita into serving dishes. Top with a dollop of Perfectly Whipped Cream

FOR Perfectly Whipped Cream: With an electric mixer, whip the cream until it starts to thicken. Add the vanilla and SomerSweet. Continue whipping until soft peaks form. **serves 6 to 8**

Chef Tip: "Granita" is the Italian word for "dessert ice." I've added heavy cream to this classic recipe to make it even smoother. Allow 3 to 4 hours to complete the granita. I use my signature sweetener, SomerSweet, but feel free to substitute sugar if you wish.

PMS Espresso-Chocolate Walnut Brownies

Karen Brooks & Diane Morgan

Vegetable-oil cooking spray
¾ cup chopped walnuts
1 cup cake flour or ¾ cup all-purpose flour
¼ cup unsweetened cocoa powder
¼ teaspoon kosher salt
¾ teaspoon baking powder
1½ tablespoons finely ground espresso beans
3 ounces unsweetened chocolate, finely chopped
¾ cup (1½ sticks) unsalted butter at room temperature
1½ cups sugar
3 large eggs, lightly beaten
1 teaspoon vanilla extract

PREHEAT the oven to 350°F. Spray an 8×8-inch baking dish with cooking spray. Line the pan with aluminum foil; then spray the foil with cooking spray.

SPREAD the walnuts on a rimmed baking sheet and toast in the oven until lightly browned, about 6 to 8 minutes. Set aside to cool.

MEANWHILE, sift together the flour, cocoa powder, salt, and baking powder into a small bowl. Stir in the ground espresso and set aside.

FILL a medium saucepan one-third full with water and bring to a simmer. Place the chocolate and butter in a large heat-proof bowl and set over the simmering water.

Turn the heat to low. Melt the chocolate and butter, stirring frequently, until completely smooth. Remove from the heat and stir in the sugar. Whisk in the eggs and vanilla. Stir in the flour mixture just until the flour is absorbed. Stir in the nuts.

POUR the batter evenly into the pan. Bake until a crust forms on top and the center is still somewhat gooey, but not *Baywatch* jiggly, about 30 to 35 minutes. Cool in the pan set on a rack. Refrigerate 2 hours. Cut into 1-inch squares to serve. **makes 64 bite-sized brownies**

Chef Tip: Keep those extra brownies in the freezer. As the crabby mood kicks in, pop one of these trufflelike gems. Better than Motrin, and twice the fun.

four

Family Gatherings

Ann Curry >

Q&A

Q. Who inspired your interest in cooking?

A. My grandmother was a wonderful cook and inspired me to love cooking as much as she did.

Q. What is your first memory of cooking?

A. My first memory of cooking is watching my grandmother Edith making doughnuts, telling me not to get too close to the pot of oil.

Q. Since you have traveled across the globe, what is your favorite regional cuisine?

A. I love food from all over the world, but one of my favorites is Mediterranean cuisine, with hummus, tabouli, kalamata olives, and feta cheese. So much flavor and wonderful spices are in this cuisine. It is a delight to eat.

Q. What meals do you make for your kids that they love?

A. They love everything. They don't have a choice.

Q. What is your favorite gourmet meal to eat or prepare?

A. Pasta Puttanesca, my own recipe. My husband teases that it's one reason why he married me.

Q. What are your favorite spices for cooking?

A. Curry, of course.

Q. What is your favorite recipe and where did you get it?

A. My Pasta Puttanesca. I got the recipe from one of my great friends, Greg Huebner, who is the sommelier at Chinois, a restaurant in Santa Monica. Then I altered it a bit, adding more garlic and using cherry tomatoes. Greg now likes my version better!

Q. What do you make when you are entertaining guests? Why?

A. Once again, I would have to say my Pasta Puttanesca because it never ever fails. I serve it with warm crusty bread to dip into garlicky olive oil.

Q. What is your favorite comfort food?

A. My favorite comfort food is chocolate. I like it dark, straight or covering dried orange rinds. To me it is the best, most blissfully perfect food ever created.

Q. What is the food that you should not eat but do?

A. I should not eat chips. No one should. But who can resist?

Q. Do you follow recipes or do you just like to experiment? Is cooking a creative process for you?

A. I experiment. The pleasure of cooking is in creating, especially when the food you make is going to be served to people you love.

Q. Has your style of cooking changed over the years? If so, what influenced the change?

A. I am a bolder cook than I once was. I am less afraid of failure ... maybe because I'm so used to it! Ha! I use more spices and herbs. And I cook and eat healthier than ever before.

Q. What do you eat for breakfast before the show?

A. I only drink coffee before the show; then I have fruit during the show. I'm not a big breakfast eater. Besides, I want to be hungry for our food segments!

Q. Tell us about a memorable moment of a Today's Kitchen segment.

A. My best memory of a kitchen segment is when Dustin Hoffman and Tim Robbins joined us for cooking pizza. The flour was flying and we laughed more than we ate.

Ann's Sugar Cookies ◀ **A**nn **C**urry

¾ cup (1½ sticks) softened
   unsalted butter
¾ cup sugar
1 large egg
1 teaspoon vanilla extract
1 tablespoon grated orange peel
2¼ cups all purpose flour
¼ teaspoon salt

For Royal Icing:
3 egg whites
1 pound confectioner's sugar
   (1 box)
   Food coloring

CREAM together butter and sugar. Add egg, vanilla and orange peel. Beat together. Add flour and salt. Roll out to a quarter-inch thickness. Cut into shapes on ungreased cooking sheet. Bake at 350°F for 10 minutes. **makes about 2 dozen 2½-inch cookies**

For the Royal Icing
MIX together egg whites and confectioner's sugar. Use food coloring if desired. Put icing on cooled cookies. The icing will harden, so if you want to add sprinkles or other decorations, do it immediately.

Baked Sweet Potato Gratin *with ginger and pineapples*

Tanya Holland

3 pounds sweet potatoes, sliced thin
2 tablespoons butter, cut into small cubes
1 cup crushed pineapple in its own juice
¼ cup minced fresh ginger
½ cup light brown sugar

PREHEAT oven to 350°F and use a 2-quart baking dish. In a small bowl mix together pineapple, ginger, and brown sugar; set aside. In the baking dish, make one layer of overlapping slices of sweet potatoes. Sprinkle with pineapple mixture, dot with butter, and then make another layer of potatoes and continue in this pattern until potatoes are finished. End with pineapple mixture and butter on top. Bake for 35 to 40 minutes, until golden brown on top. **serves 8**

Chef Tip: Choose sweet potatoes that have as few bruises as possible. The skin should be smooth and not bumpy.

Curtis Aikens > Mama's Collard Greens

4 bunches collards, stemmed, washed very well, and torn into small pieces
2¼ cups water
¼ cup olive or vegetable oil*
Light salt and pepper to taste
1 onion, cut in half or diced
3 cloves of garlic, sliced
½ green bell pepper, julienned

COOK all ingredients together about 2 hours or until greens are tender.

serves 4 to 6

*VARY** according to individual preference (lower-fat diets use less).

Chef Tip: If you remove the big stems from the collard leaves, you can cut your cooking time by 35 to 45 minutes. How? Fold the leaf along the stem line, then pull it off.

Cold Potato Salad ◀ Maya Angelou

6 cups peeled, diced,
    cooked potatoes
1 medium onion, finely chopped
1 cup finely diced celery
1 cup chopped dill pickles
1 cup sweet relish, drained
8 large hard-boiled eggs,
    4 chopped, 4 whole
    Salt and freshly ground black
    pepper to taste
1¼ cups mayonnaise
    Fresh parsley, chopped

COMBINE potatoes, onion, celery, pickles, relish, and chopped eggs. Season with salt and pepper, and add mayonnaise. Chill for several hours. Just before serving, halve the remaining 4 eggs, and place on salad as decoration. Dust salad with parsley, and serve at once.

serves 6 to 8

Chef Tip: To prepare the potatoes, cook them until done but still firm. Remove the potatoes from the water and place in a plastic bag; let cool on the kitchen counter. Peel the cooled potatoes and dice. Sprinkle with salt and a teaspoon of olive oil; mix well.

Mama's Corn Bread ◀ **C**urtis **A**ikens

1½ cups cornmeal
½ cup flour
1 cup buttermilk
2 large eggs
2 teaspoons baking powder
½ teaspoon baking soda
6 tablespoons vegetable oil

PREHEAT the oven to 375°F. In a mixing bowl, combine all of the ingredients except oil and mix well. On the stove top, heat the oil in a large skillet until hot but not boiling. Pour the hot oil into the bowl with the other ingredients and mix well. Pour the batter into the skillet and bake for 35 to 50 minutes. Start checking for doneness after 35 minutes; it should be golden brown when done.

serves 4 to 6

Chef Tip: The best corn bread is made in cast-iron skillets. So if you do not have one, get one!

Tyler Florence > ## Soft Polenta

with parmesan and black pepper

2 quarts chicken stock
1 teaspoon sea salt
2 cups polenta or yellow cornmeal
⅓ cup heavy cream
2 tablespoons unsalted butter, at room temperature
1 cup freshly grated Parmigiano-Reggiano cheese
1½ teaspoons freshly ground black pepper

IN a large pot, bring the chicken stock and salt to a boil. Gradually whisk in the cornmeal in a slow, steady stream. The liquid will be absorbed and the cornmeal will lock up; don't freak, just whisk through it. Lower the heat and continue to whisk until the polenta is thick and smooth, about 20 minutes. Add the cream and butter; continue to stir until incorporated, about 10 minutes. Remove from the heat, fold in the Parmigiano and black pepper, and serve. **serves 6**

Black-Eyed Peas ◄ Curtis Aikens

1 pound dried black-eyed
   peas, soaked overnight
½ stick (2 ounces) butter
   or margarine
1 large onion, cut into big cubes
1 large shallot, quartered
3 to 4 cups water
¼ green bell pepper, cored,
   seeded and chopped
1 teaspoon salt
½ teaspoon freshly ground
   black pepper
¼ cup oil*

DRAIN the peas, discarding the water, and set them aside. In a large skillet over medium heat, put the butter, onion and shallot. When the butter is melted, increase the heat and add the peas. Mix with a wooden spoon, cover and cook about 8 minutes. Pour the contents of the skillet into a large pot, adding enough water to cover the peas. Bring to a boil, and add green bell pepper, salt and black pepper.

Lower the heat to medium and cook 50 to 60 minutes, or until peas are tender. **serves 4 to 6**

*VARY according to individual preference (lower-fat diets use less).

Chef Tip: About 50 minutes into cooking, take out ½ cup of the peas and mash them up, add back to pot, and stir. This gives the peas a smooth texture that I love and hope you will also.

Charlie Palmer's Super Bowl Soup

Charlie Palmer

¾ cup dried small white beans
¾ cup dried pinto beans
3 tablespoons olive oil
2 large onions, peeled and chopped
2 cloves garlic, peeled and chopped
12 ounces hot, spicy sausage, cut crosswise into ½-inch pieces
2 bay leaves
1 tablespoon chile powder
8 cups nonfat, low-sodium chicken broth
6 large button mushrooms, cleaned and diced
5 small red bliss potatoes, well-washed and diced
3 plum tomatoes, well washed, cored, seeded and diced
¼ pound fresh escarole, well washed and chopped
Coarse salt and freshly ground pepper to taste
3 tablespoons chopped fresh flat-leaf parsley
1 tablespoon chopped fresh basil
1 cup cooked toasted barley (optional)

PLACE the beans in a large bowl with cold water to cover by 2 inches. Set aside to soak overnight or at least 8 hours.

WHEN ready to cook, heat the olive oil in a large, heavy bottom casserole-type pan over medium heat. Add the onions and garlic and sauté for 10 minutes or until just slightly colored. Add the sausage and sauté for an additional 5 minutes.

DRAIN the beans and add them to the pot along with the bay leaves and chile powder. Add the broth, raise the heat and bring to a boil. Lower the heat and cook at a gentle simmer for 20 minutes.

STIR in the mushrooms, potatoes, tomatoes and escarole and again bring to a boil. Lower the heat and simmer for 40 minutes or until the beans are tender.

SEASON with salt and pepper to taste. Stir in the parsley and basil and remove from the heat.

SERVE, piping hot, with toasted barley sprinkled over the top for crunchiness; serve hard pretzels and ice cold beer on the side.

makes enough for a crowd

Chef Tip: If you don't have the time to soak the dried beans, you can substitute with canned beans. Replace ¾ cup dried beans with 2 cups of canned beans, drained, and add halfway through the 40 minutes of simmering.

Suzanne Somers > Caesar Salad

4 anchovies
1 teaspoon cracked black
  peppercorns
1/3 cup extra virgin olive oil
1/2 cup freshly grated
  Parmesan cheese
1 egg
3 tablespoons red wine vinegar
2 tablespoons fresh lemon juice
1 tablespoon pureed garlic
2 teaspoons dry mustard
1 teaspoon celery salt
3 dashes Tabasco
3 dashes Worcestershire sauce
2 medium heads Romaine lettuce

COMBINE anchovies, black pepper and olive oil in a blender. Puree until very smooth, about 5 minutes. Add grated Parmesan and blend briefly to combine.

BRING a small saucepan of water to a boil. Place a refrigerated egg on a slotted spoon and into boiling water. Cook 1 1/2 minutes, remove and reserve.

PLACE remaining dressing ingredients into a large bowl and whisk in anchovy mixture. Crack open egg and spoon (including the parts that are uncooked) into mixture. Whisk until well combined. The dressing may be refrigerated at this stage.

WASH and dry lettuce. Arrange lettuce spears onto serving plates and drizzle dressing over the top. Garnish with shaved Parmesan and serve. serves 6

Chef Tip: The presentation of spears dripping with sauce is beautiful; however, you may break the lettuce into bite-size pieces if you find it easier to serve. This dressing is my all-time favorite—a really traditional tableside Caesar.

Salad of Endive,
roasted pears and toasted walnuts

Tyler Florence

3 bartlett pears, cored and halved
2/3 cup extra-virgin olive oil
1/2 cup walnuts, shelled
4 endive, washed, dried and chopped
1 pint mâche
1 tablespoon fresh lemon juice
1 tablespoon honey
1 tablespoon mustard
2 tablespoons cider vinegar
Sea salt and freshly ground black pepper

PREHEAT the oven to 350°F. Drizzle 1/3 cup of the olive oil onto the pears and season with salt and pepper. Place cut side down on a sheet pan and roast for 20 minutes. Remove the pears from oven and set aside to cool. Place the walnuts on a pan and toast in the oven for 3 to 5 minutes.

IN a mixing bowl, whisk together the remaining oil, lemon juice, honey, mustard and cider vinegar. Season well with salt and pepper. Slice the pear halves into 4 slices each.

PLACE the endive, pears, mâche and walnuts in a large serving bowl, Toss gently with dressing and serve.
serves 6 to 8 (appetizer servings)

Pork Tenderloin
with mango salsa and blackberry syrup

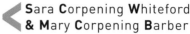

Sara Corpening Whiteford
& Mary Corpening Barber

For Mango Salsa:
- 1½ cups diced mango (about 1 large mango)
- 2 tablespoons finely chopped red onion
- 1 tablespoon chopped fresh mint
- ½ teaspoon chopped jalapeño chile, seeded and deribbed, plus more as needed
- ½ teaspoon grated lime zest
- 2 teaspoons fresh lime juice, plus more as needed
- ¼ teaspoon kosher salt, plus more as needed

For Blackberry Syrup:
- ¾ cup raspberry vinegar
- 3 tablespoons seedless blackberry preserves
- ⅛ teaspoon kosher salt

For Pork Tenderloins:
- 2 pork tenderloins (about 12 ounces each)
- 1¼ teaspoons kosher salt
- ½ teaspoon freshly ground pepper
- 2 tablespoons vegetable oil
- Mint sprigs for garnishing

PREHEAT the oven to 450°F. Line a baking sheet with aluminum foil.

TO make the mango salsa: Combine the mango, red onion, mint, jalapeño, lime zest, lime juice, and kosher salt in a medium bowl. Season with more jalapeño, lime juice, and kosher salt if necessary. Let stand, covered, at room temperature.

TO make the blackberry syrup: Put the vinegar in a small saucepan over low heat and simmer until reduced to about 2 tablespoons, about 3 minutes. Whisk in the preserves and kosher salt until smooth. Cover and keep warm.

SEASON the pork with the kosher salt and pepper. Heat the oil in a 12-inch heavy skillet over high heat and sauté the pork, turning as

needed, until golden, 2 to 3 minutes per side. Transfer to the prepared baking sheet. Place in the oven and roast until pork is just cooked through but is still pink in the center, 8 to 12 minutes. An instant-read thermometer inserted into the center of the meat should register 150°F.

TRANSFER the pork to a cutting board and let rest for at least 5 minutes, then slice on the diagonal. Fan the slices on a serving plate, top with the mango salsa, and drizzle with the blackberry syrup. Garnish with mint sprigs.
serves 3 to 4

Chef Tip: The salsa may be made up to 1 day in advance and refrigerated. Bring to room temperature before serving. When sweet tasting mangoes are difficult to find, we often substitute fresh white peaches, nectarines, plums, or pineapple.

Suzanne Somers > Somersize Mac and Cheese

Butter for greasing baking dish
8 egg crepes, sliced into
  1/4-inch strips
4 cups heavy cream
2 1/2 cups shredded cheddar cheese
Pinch nutmeg
Pinch ground red pepper
Salt and pepper

For the Egg Crepes:
6 eggs
Salt and freshly ground
  black pepper
Butter

PREHEAT the oven to 350 degrees. Butter an 8×8-inch glass baking dish. Set aside.

PLACE cream in a heavy medium saucepan. Bring to a boil, reduce heat slightly and let boil gently for 10 minutes, or until reduced by half. Lower heat and add 1 1/2 cups cheddar cheese, nutmeg and ground red pepper. Stir until cheese melts and sauce is smooth.

PLACE sliced egg crepes in prepared baking dish. Pour sauce over crepes and stir to coat. Top with remaining cheese. Bake for 20 minutes, or until cheese is bubbly and beginning to brown. Serve hot. **serves 4**

For the Egg Crepes:
IN a mixing bowl, lightly beat the eggs. Season with salt and pepper. Heat a crepe or omelette pan over medium to medium-high heat and lightly coat the bottom and sides with butter. Using a ladle, put enough egg in the pan to make a thin coating. When it sets, lift up with a spatula, being careful not to tear the crepe, and turn. Cook one more minute and then slide the crepe out of the pan and onto a dish. Continue making egg crepes in this way until you have used all the batter. Stack the crepes as you would pancakes.

Chef Tip: Who says macaroni and cheese needs to come in a box! And who says it even needs macaroni? I use Egg Crepes to make Somersize "noodles." This is a great dish to make ahead of time, but reheat in the oven, not the microwave, or the cream will separate.

Bow Tie Pasta
with asparagus, sun-dried tomatoes, and boursin

Sara **C**orpening **W**hiteford & **M**ary **C**orpening **B**arber

1/3 cup pine nuts
Kosher salt
8 ounces bow tie pasta
14 medium spears asparagus, peeled and cut into 1½-inch pieces
1 tablespoon olive oil
4 large cloves garlic, minced
1/3 cup drained, oil-packed sun-dried tomatoes, chopped
1/4 cup grated Parmesan cheese, preferably Parmigiano-Reggiano
2 ounces (1/3 cup) garlic and fine herbs Boursin
1 tablespoon chopped fresh dill, or 3/4 teaspoon dried dill weed
3/4 teaspoon lemon pepper, plus more as needed
Fresh flat-leaf parsley leaves for garnishing (optional)

PUT the pine nuts in a small skillet over medium heat. Shake constantly until evenly toasted on all sides, about 4 minutes. Set aside.

FILL a large saucepan three-fourths full of water. Bring to a boil over high heat and add kosher salt. (We add 1½ teaspoons kosher salt per quart of water.) Add the pasta and cook, stirring occasionally, until barely tender, 8 to 10 minutes. Add the asparagus to the pan and cook until tender-crisp, 1 to 2 minutes. Drain the pasta and asparagus, reserving 3/4 cup of the cooking water. Set the pan over medium heat and heat the olive oil. Add the garlic and cook until lightly brown,

1 to 2 minutes. Return the pasta and asparagus to the pan, then add the reserved cooking water. Add the tomatoes, Parmesan cheese, Boursin, dill and the 3/4 teaspoon lemon pepper and toss to combine. Season with kosher salt to taste and more lemon pepper if necessary.

DIVIDE the pasta between 2 bowls and garnish with parsley, if desired. Serve immediately. **serves 2**

Chef Tip: Our secret to this simple fare is the Boursin, a creamy French cheese flavored with garlic and herbs. If you have some left over, stir a dollop into scrambled eggs, smear onto a toasted bagel, or spread onto raw vegetables!

Perfect Roast Chicken ◄ **C**harlie **P**almer

1   6-pound roasting chicken
     (free-range preferred)
1   lemon
1   large onion, peeled (or 1 large
     lemon, orange or apple,
     unpeeled)
1   sprig fresh rosemary, optional
     Coarse salt and freshly ground
     pepper to taste
½   cup dry white wine or water
1   tablespoon cornstarch
     dissolved in 1 tablespoon
     cold water, optional
1   cup chicken broth (or more
     as needed), optional

PREHEAT the oven to 450°F. Rinse the chicken under cool running water. Drain well and pat dry. Reserve the giblets for another use, if desired.

CUT the lemon in half, crosswise, and squeeze the juice directly onto the chicken skin, rubbing it in as you squeeze. Cover all of the skin with lemon juice. Place the onion (or fruit) into the cavity along with the optional sprig of rosemary. Season the cavity with salt and pepper to taste. Fasten the neck skin under the chicken with a small skewer. Close the cavity with a skewer or by sewing closed with a larding needle and thread. Fold the wing tips under the wings. Generously season the outside of the chicken with salt and pepper.

PLACE the chicken on a rack in a heavy roasting pan. Push the legs back against the body but don't tie them together as this will keep the meat from roasting evenly. Pour the wine or water into the roasting pan and place the pan into the preheated oven. Roast for 30 minutes. Lower the heat to 375°F and continue to roast for about an additional hour or until the chicken skin is golden-brown and crisp, the thigh meat is soft to the touch and an instant-read thermometer inserted into the thickest part of the breast reads 155°F.

REMOVE the chicken from the oven and let it stand for 5 minutes. Carve and, if desired, serve with gravy on the side.

TO carve chicken: To remove the wings, slice at the base joint against the body. Set aside. Pull legs slightly away from the body. Slice down through the thigh joint to separate entire leg from the body. Slice through the leg joint to divide the drumstick from the thigh. With the knife parallel to the breast bone, slice the breast meat away from the carcass by cutting from the center of the breast slightly to the front,

removing the meat in thin slices. Alternately, remove the entire breast by carefully cutting it away from the breast bone and then cutting the breast meat, crosswise, into thin slices. If desired, you can remove the skin from the chicken before slicing it by gently lifting it up and away from the meat.

IF gravy is desired, drain excess fat from the roasting pan after the chicken and rack have been removed. Place the pan on the top of the stove over medium heat. (This may require 2 burners.) Stir the optional cornstarch dissolved in water and the chicken broth into the pan juices. Bring to a boil and cook, stirring constantly, for about 5 minutes or until the gravy is smooth and the starchiness has cooked out. Taste and adjust the seasoning with salt and pepper. Serve hot. **serves 6**

Chef Tip: My secret to the perfect roast chicken is lemon juice. It seals in the meat juices, helps crisp and brown the skin, and, if you roast a whole lemon in the cavity, chopped, it will make a great condiment for the finished plate.

Maya Angelou > Chicken and Dumplings

Chicken:
- 1 whole chicken (about 4 pounds cut up)
- 6 chicken wings
- 1 large Spanish onion, chopped and sautéed but not browned
- 2 stalks celery, chopped
- 1 carrot, peeled and chopped
- 1 green bell pepper, chopped
  Bouquet Garni (recipe follows)
  Salt and freshly ground black pepper, to taste
  Drop Dumplings (recipe follows)

Drop Dumplings:
- 2 cups sifted all-purpose flour
- 1/4 teaspoon salt
- 2 heaping teaspoons baking powder
- 2 tablespoons (1/4 stick) butter
- 1 cup plus 2 tablespoons milk

For the Chicken

WASH and pat dry chicken. Take flange off chicken wings.

PLACE cut-up chicken and wings into large, heavy pot, and add water to cover 1 inch above chicken. Add onion, celery, carrot, bell pepper, and Bouquet Garni. Season with salt and pepper. Allow mixture to simmer slowly for 1½ hours. Let cool. Remove any foam that has gathered on top of the broth.

BRING broth to a slight boil, and drop heaping tablespoons of dumpling batter into pot. Fill top of pot with dumplings. Cover pot, and simmer for 15 minutes—dumplings will rise. Baste dumplings, and continue simmering for another 5 minutes. Remove cover and baste dumplings. Serve hot on platter.

serves 6 to 8

For the Dumplings

SIFT flour, salt, and baking powder into mixing bowl. Add butter, mixing with fingertips, then milk, until mixture is consistency of grainy cornmeal.

For the Bouquet Garni: Cut double thickness of cheesecloth 6 inches wide. Place 3 bay leaves, 8 black peppercorns, tops from two stalks of celery, and 1 teaspoon margarine in center of cheesecloth. Pull corners of cheesecloth together, and tie with kitchen twine.

Chef Tip: After 15 minutes of cooking, carefully turn the dumplings over into the hot broth. Cover and return to low until dumplings are done.

Mama's Fried Chicken ◀ **C**urtis **A**ikens

**Whole chicken, cut into pieces
(or you can use chicken parts)**
½ **to 1 cup buttermilk**
Salt and pepper
1½ **cup self-rising flour**
**Oil for frying (Wesson
vegetable oil)**

WASH chicken pieces. Sprinkle with salt and pepper to taste. Marinate 1 hour in buttermilk. Roll pieces in flour and deep fry until golden brown. **serves 4 to 6**

Chef Tip: If you want, marinate the chicken overnight and all day while you are at work. Add ½ teaspoon of salt and black pepper—the chicken will be even juicier.

Meatball Lasagna ◀ Scotto Family

For the Meatballs:
- 2 slices bread
- ½ cup milk
- 2 pounds ground beef
- 1 cup finely chopped onions
- 3 tablespoons chopped fresh parsley
- 2 eggs
- 4 tablespoons grated Parmesan cheese
- 1½ tablespoons chopped garlic
  Salt and pepper
- 3 tablespoons olive oil
- 5 cups tomato sauce, warmed

For the Lasagna:
- 2 pounds fresh mozzarella, diced
- 2 cups grated Parmigiano-Reggiano cheese
- 5 pounds fresh ricotta cheese
- 3 eggs
- ½ cup chopped fresh parsley
  Salt and pepper
- 4 fresh pasta sheets (store-bought) or 2 pounds lasagna noodles

TO make the meatballs: Soak the bread in the milk. In a medium bowl, mix the ground beef, bread, onions, parsley, eggs, cheese, and garlic. Add salt and pepper to taste. If the mixture is dry, add ½ cup of cold water and mix well. Form into about 12 meatballs. Place the meatballs in a sauté pan with the olive oil and fry over medium to high heat until brown, 10 to 15 minutes. Drain the meatballs on paper towels.

IN a stockpot, heat the tomato sauce over low heat. Add the meatballs to the sauce and simmer over low heat, covered, for 30 minutes, or until meatballs are cooked through. Remove from the heat and set aside.

TO make the lasagna: Mix ¾ of the mozzarella, 1 cup of the Parmigiano-Reggiano, and the ricotta in a large bowl. Add the eggs and parsley. Season with salt and pepper and set aside. Remove the meatballs from the sauce. Crumble the meatballs and set aside.

BRING a large pot of salted water to a boil over high heat and cook the pasta until al dente, about 1 minute. Drain and shock in cold water.

TO assemble: Preheat the oven to 350°F. Pour 1 cup of the hot tomato sauce in the bottom of an 8×12-inch baking pan. Place a pasta sheet over the layer of sauce, cutting the sheet to fit if necessary.

SPREAD ⅓ of the cheese mixture over the pasta. Spread ⅓ of the crumbled meatballs over the cheese. Add some of the sauce and sprinkle with the remaining ¼ of the mozzarella and Parmesan. Repeat the layers of sauce, pasta, cheese, and meatballs two more times.

SPREAD the remaining cup of tomato sauce over the top layer of the pasta and sprinkle the remaining Parmigiano-Reggiano cheese over the sauce.

BAKE the lasagna for 1 hour or until the top is golden.
serves 8 to 10

Chef Tip: Be sure to use the best quality cheese available.

Country Plum Cake ◄ Jacques **Pépin**

Cake:
- 1 cup all-purpose flour (5½ ounces)
- 1 cup whole almonds (5½ ounces)
- ⅔ cup sugar
- 1 teaspoon double-acting baking powder
- 1 teaspoon vanilla extract
- ½ stick (2 ounces) unsalted butter, softened (with ¼ teaspoon reserved for buttering the mold)
- 2 tablespoons canola oil
- 2 large eggs
- ⅓ cup milk

Garnishes:
- 4 to 6 ripe plums, preferably Black Friar or Santa Rosa (1¼ pounds)
- 3 tablespoons sugar
- ½ cup plum jam
- 1 tablespoon plum brandy or Cognac

PREHEAT the oven to 350°F. For the cake: Place the flour, almonds, and ⅔ cup sugar in the bowl of a food processor and process until the mixture is a coarse powder. Add the baking powder, vanilla, butter (minus ¼ teaspoon), oil, and eggs and process for a few seconds, just until incorporated.

ADD the milk, and process for an additional few seconds, until the mixture is smooth. Use the reserved ¼ teaspoon of butter to coat the inside of a 10-inch springform mold. Pour in the batter. (It should be about ¾ inch thick in the mold.)

FOR the garnishes: Using the point of a sharp knife, remove the pit from the stem hole of each plum. Rinse the whole pitted plums well in cold water, and, while they are still wet, roll them in the 3 tablespoons of sugar. (If the plums are not fully ripened and feel hard, prick them all over with the point of a sharp

knife to soften them before rolling them in the sugar.) Arrange the plums on top of the cake, spacing them evenly, and push them down into the batter until the bottom half of each is immersed.

PLACE the cake on a cookie sheet and bake in the center of the oven for 40 minutes, or until puffy and nicely browned on top. Cool on a rack until lukewarm.

MIX the plum jam and the brandy together in a small bowl and brush the top of the lukewarm cake with the mixture. Remove the cake from the mold and cut it into six wedges so that each serving contains one plum. Serve while still lukewarm or just at room temperature. **serves 6**

Chef Tip: If baked without the fruit garnish, the cake freezes well. (The fruit would become soggy and mushy when the dessert thaws.) For best results, wrap the cake in plastic wrap and aluminum foil before freezing it and defrost in the refrigerator while still wrapped.

Buttermilk Cake ◄ Sara Foster
with fresh strawberries and cream

4¹/₂ cups all-purpose flour
1 tablespoon baking powder
1 teaspoon baking soda
¹/₂ teaspoon salt
³/₄ pound (3 sticks) unsalted butter
2¹/₂ cups granulated sugar
6 large eggs
2 teaspoons pure vanilla extract
2 cups buttermilk
3 cups heavy cream
3 pints fresh strawberries, hulled and cut into ¹/₂-inch lengthwise slices
1 pint fresh strawberries, hulled

PREHEAT oven to 325°F. Grease and lightly flour two 9-inch round or square cake pans, 2 inches deep, and set aside.

SIFT together the flour, baking powder, baking soda and salt in a bowl and stir again to mix. Set aside.

CREAM together butter and 2¹/₄ cups of the sugar in a separate bowl with an electric mixer.

ADD eggs, one at a time, to the butter mixture and beat several minutes until light and fluffy. Add vanilla and stir by hand to mix.

ADD buttermilk to the flour mixture, alternating with egg mixture, and stir until well combined.

DIVIDE the batter evenly between the prepared pans and bake 45 to 50 minutes, until cakes are firm to touch and a toothpick inserted into the center of each cake comes out clean.

REMOVE from the oven and cool the cakes 10 to 15 minutes in the pans. Remove from pans and continue to

cool on a baking rack. Once the cakes have cooled completely, use a serrated knife to slice off the top rounded part of each layer to make a flat, even surface. Cut each layer in half horizontally through the center to make four layers. Discard the trimmings.

MEANWHILE, whip the cream in a bowl with remaining ¹/₄ cup sugar until soft peaks form.

PLACE one layer, cut side down, on a cake plate. Top with about one-third of the whipped cream and one-third of the sliced berries. Repeat the process with the next two layers and the remaining cream and sliced berries. Place the fourth layer on top, cut side down. Top with the whole hulled berries and sprinkle with confectioners' sugar just before serving. (Note: If you are going to refrigerate the cake, add the confectioners' sugar just before serving. This cake can be refrigerated up to 1 day ahead.)
makes one 9-inch cake

Chef Tip: Make the layers a day ahead of time, wrap in plastic wrap, and assemble the morning before serving.

Maya Angelou > Caramel Cake

8 tablespoons (1 stick) butter
1¼ cups sugar
¼ cup Caramel Syrup
   (recipe follows)
2 cups sifted all-purpose flour
2 teaspoons baking powder
½ teaspoon salt
1 cup milk
2 large eggs
   Caramel Frosting (recipe follows)

Caramel Syrup
1 cup white sugar
1 cup boiling water

Caramel Frosting
6 tablespoons (¾ stick) butter
1 8-ounce package
   confectioners' sugar
4 tablespoons heavy cream
1½ teaspoons vanilla extract
   Pinch of salt

PREHEAT oven to 375°F. Line two 8-inch layer cake pans with greased wax paper.

IN large mixing bowl, beat butter, and add 1 cup sugar gradually until light and fluffy. Beat in syrup.

IN medium mixing bowl, sift flour, baking powder, and salt together. Add sifted ingredients to creamed mixture, alternating with milk.

IN separate medium mixing bowl, beat eggs about 3 minutes, until foamy. Add remaining sugar, and beat until there is a fine spongy foam. Stir into cake batter until blended.

DIVIDE batter between cake pans. Bake for about 25 minutes. Remove pans from oven. Gently press center of cake with forefinger. Cake should spring back when finger is removed. If it doesn't, return to oven for 10 minutes. Cool in pans for 10 minutes. Turn out onto rack, and remove wax paper. Let cakes cool to room temperature before frosting.

TO ASSEMBLE: Center one cooled cake layer on cake plate. Cover top and sides with generous helping of frosting. Place second layer evenly on frosted layer. Repeat frosting procedure. Make certain that sides are completely frosted. Cool in refrigerator until ready to serve. serves 8

For the Caramel Syrup
HEAT sugar in heavy skillet over low heat. Stir constantly until melted to a brown liquid. When it bubbles over entire surface, remove from heat. Slowly add boiling water, stirring constantly. Pour into container and cool.

For the Caramel Frosting
BROWN butter in heavy pot over medium heat—be vigilant or it will burn. Allow butter to cool. In large mixing bowl, add confectioners' sugar, cream, vanilla extract, and salt to the butter, and beat until smooth. If frosting is too stiff, add tablespoon of half-and-half or full cream to thin.

Chef Tip: Spread raspberry preserves on the cake layers before the Caramel Frosting.

Almond and Bittersweet Chocolate Fondue

◄ **C**harlie **P**almer

10 ounces bittersweet
     chocolate (60%)
 3 tablespoons cocoa powder,
     sifted
 1 tablespoon butter
 ½ cup amaretto
 ¾ cup heavy cream, warm
 ¾ cup milk, warm
 1 cup sugar

Garnishes:
     Toasted chunks of nut bread
     Pound cakes, cut into medium
       sized cubes
     Banana, sliced
     Candied ginger or citrus fruit
     Strawberries
     Marshmallows

PLACE the chopped bittersweet chocolate into a bowl and sift the cocoa powder over. Add the butter to the bowl and melt all together over a double boiler.

HEAT the milk, cream, amaretto, and sugar together in a small pot. Bring to a simmer and then remove from the fire; stir to make sure all of the sugar has dissolved.

WHISK the cream mixture into the melted chocolate and then transfer to a fondue pot.

SERVE with garnishes. serves 6

Chef Tip: If your fondue breaks (fat separates from chocolate), don't panic. Just whisk in a small amount of cold heavy cream (1 ounce to start) and your perfect fondue is back. If you have leftovers, let the fondue harden, roll spoonfuls into bite-size balls, and coat with cocoa powder. You now have chocolate truffles!

Mexican Banana Split ◄ Ivy Stark

1 quart coffee ice cream
1 quart chocolate ice cream
1 quart peanut butter ice cream
1 cup Chocolate Kahlua Sauce
   (recipe follows)
1 cup Cajeta (recipe follows)
2 ripe bananas
   Banana Churros
   (recipe follows)
   Whipped cream
   Chopped toasted peanuts

Chocolate Kahlua Sauce
4 ounces bittersweet or
   unsweetened Mexican
   chocolate, chopped
1/2 cup heavy cream
1/4 cup kahlua

PLACE chocolate in a bowl. Bring the cream and the kahlua to a boil and pour over chocolate, stirring until combined. Keep warm.

Cajeta
1 quart goat's milk or cow's milk
1 cup sugar
1 teaspoon pure vanilla extract

PLACE all ingredients in a heavy-bottomed saucepan and bring to a boil. Reduce heat to simmer and allow to reduce to a thick caramel, stirring frequently to avoid burning. Strain and keep warm.

Banana Churros
1/4 cup water
2 ounces butter
3/4 cup milk
2 cups all-purpose flour
1 teaspoon baking powder
2 eggs
1 very ripe banana, mashed
1 tablespoon sugar
1 teaspoon ground cinnamon

BRING the water, butter and milk to a boil. Add the flour and baking powder, stirring rapidly until a soft ball is formed and dough pulls away from the sides of the pan. With an electric mixer, beat in the eggs one at a time and then add the banana. Allow to cool for a few minutes and pipe into 2 inch tubes with a pastry bag filled with a star tip. Fry in 350°F oil until golden brown. Combine the cinnamon and sugar. While the churros are still warm, dust with cinnamon sugar.

TO ASSEMBLE:
SLICE the bananas into long strips on the bias and sauté in a little bit of butter until golden brown. Lay the banana strips in the bottom of four serving dishes.

PLACE one scoop of each ice cream in each serving dish, and pour the sauces over the ice cream.

TOP with the whipped cream, toasted peanuts and warm banana churros. **serves 4**

Charlie Palmer > Summer Berry Trifle

2 pints fresh raspberries,
  washed and patted dry
2 pints fresh strawberries,
  washed, stemmed, patted
  dry and quartered
1¼ cups sugar
2 tablespoons fresh lemon juice
1 cup seedless raspberry jam
2 pints fresh blueberries,
  washed and patted dry
3 cups heavy cream, chilled
1 teaspoon pure vanilla extract
48 ladyfingers
49 fresh mint sprigs for garnish

COMBINE the raspberries and strawberries in a mixing bowl. Sprinkle ½ cup of the sugar and 1½ tablespoons of the lemon juice over the berries. Add the jam and gently toss to coat. Set aside for 30 minutes.

PLACE the blueberries in another mixing bowl. Sprinkle with ½ cup of the remaining sugar and the remaining ½ tablespoon of lemon juice and gently toss to coat. Set aside for 30 minutes.

WHEN ready to assemble the trifle, place the heavy cream in the bowl of a heavy-duty mixer. Add the remaining ¼ cup of sugar and the vanilla and beat until stiff peaks form.

PLACE 16 ladyfingers or whatever number is necessary to completely cover the bottom of a large glass trifle (or other) bowl. Spoon 2½ cups of the red fruit mixture over the bottom layer of lady fingers. Top with 2 cups of the whipped cream. Repeat the layering using all of the blueberries and half of the remaining ladyfingers and cream.

MAKE a final layer with the remaining ladyfingers, red fruits and cream. Cover with plastic film and refrigerate for at least 2 hours or up to 6 hours before serving.

SERVE chilled, garnished with fresh mint sprigs. **serves 8 to 10**

Chef Tip: If your local grocery store doesn't have ladyfingers, you can always use pound cake. Be sure to cut the pound cake into pieces the same size as the ladyfingers (3×1-inches).

Strawberry Ice Cream Sandwiches ◀ Todd English

For Strawberry, Brown Sugar and Sour Cream Ice Cream:
1¼ cups sour cream
½ cups powdered sugar
1 tablespoon fresh lemon juice
1½ teaspoons vanilla extract
1¼ cups brown sugar
6 large egg yolks
2 cups whipping cream
1 cup whole milk
1½ cups chopped fresh strawberries

For Crispy Chocolate Cookies:
4 ounces unsalted butter (1 stick)
⅓ cup powdered sugar
½ teaspoon salt
½ teaspoon vanilla extract
¾ cup flour
¼ cup cocoa

For Chocolate Coating:
16 ounces good quality semi sweet chocolate

For White Chocolate Flakes:
8 ounce "chunk" of good quality white chocolate—place in refrigerator

Strawberry, Brown Sugar and Sour Cream Ice Cream
WHISK sour cream, powdered sugar, lemon juice and vanilla in small bowl to blend. Cover; refrigerate until ready to use.

WHISK 1¼ cups brown sugar and yolks in medium bowl to blend. Bring cream and milk to simmer in large saucepan. Gradually whisk hot cream mixture into yolk mixture; return to same saucepan. Stir over medium heat until custard thickens and leaves path on back of spoon when finger is drawn across, about 5 minutes (do not boil). Pour into large bowl. Refrigerate until cool, whisking occasionally, about 45 minutes.

COMBINE sour cream mixture with macerated strawberries. Process custard in ice cream maker according to manufacturer's instructions. Fold in chopped strawberries; transfer to a bowl; cover and freeze.

Crispy Chocolate Cookies
CREAM the butter and sugar. Add vanilla extract. In a small separate bowl, combine remaining dry ingredients. Stir into butter mixture—just until incorporated, being careful not to overwork.

USING a small spoon, drop small rounds of the batter onto a prepared cookie sheet about 2 inches apart. Bake at 325°F for approximately 6 minutes, turn, and continue baking for an additional 2 minutes until crispy.

Chocolate Coating
MELT in double boiler. Remove from heat and let cool to thicken.

White Chocolate Flakes
GRATE or peel chunks with a vegetable peeler. Keep in refrigerator until needed.

TO ASSEMBLE: Sandwich ice cream between two cookies, dip dessert in chocolate coating and then roll with white chocolate flakes. **serves 4**

Chef Tip: Let sandwiches firm in the freezer before dipping in chocolate.

Peppermint Ice Cream ◄ Todd English

4 cups half-and-half
2 cups cream
1½ cups sugar
8 large egg yolks
1 small bunch fresh black peppermint or chocolate mint, chopped
1 teaspoon salt
1 vanilla bean scraped then chopped
5 peppermint candies, crushed

IN a pot combine half-and-half, heavy cream, sugar, chopped mint and vanilla bean; bring to a boil, then remove from heat and let steep 2 hours. In a bowl combine your egg yolks and salt, place your liquid back on the stove and return it to the boil. Quickly pour your liquid over your egg yolks all the while stirring until incorporated. Strain through a fine sieve and allow to cool in an ice water bath.

WHEN your peppermint custard has cooled, transfer it to your ice cream machine and process according to manufacturer's instructions; when finished, transfer to a bowl and fold in your crushed peppermint candies. Store in a clean container and freeze until firm. **serves 4**

Chef Tip: For a stronger ice cream, allow ingredients to steep overnight.

five

Holiday Menus

holiday
memories

with Katie, Matt, Al & Ann

Q. What is your favorite holiday food or recipe?

Katie Couric I love my mom's pears and Jell-O. We have it almost every Thanksgiving and Christmas. It tastes good, but what I really like is what it symbolizes: time with my family and the holidays.

Matt Lauer I could eat turkey three times a week. I love it for all holidays and especially look forward to the leftovers.

Al Roker My mother's Sweet Potato Poon. A crustless sweet potato pie, it's topped with browned marshmallows that my mother invariably forgets under the broiler and before you know it, the smoke detector is blaring.

Ann Curry Christmas sugar cookies.

Q. What Christmas gift do you remember most from childhood?

Katie Couric A tetherball set. We put it in the backyard in the hole that held my Mom's clothesline and we would play for hours.

Matt Lauer My dad was in the bicycle business, so I remember getting bikes the most. Whatever the newest model was, I'd get to test-market it with my friends, so even in the winter I was riding bikes around.

Al Roker A Motorific Torture Track. It was an obstacle course race set!

Ann Curry A brown velvet dress that my mother made.

Q. If you're invited to a holiday meal what do you bring?

Katie Couric A bottle of wine and some Christmas cookies I made with my daughters.

Matt Lauer Dessert, a cake, or pastry.

Al Roker A nice bottle of wine and an exploding wheel of cheese!

Ann Curry A spinach and pomegranate salad.

Q. How do you like to ring in the New Year?

Katie Couric Quietly and away from the crowds, almost always with my girls.

Matt Lauer We go out with another couple for a great quiet dinner to toast the New Year.

Al Roker Asleep.

Ann Curry I like to go to bed early after a nice meal with my family and feel great on the first day of the New Year.

Q. What do you like in your Easter basket?

Katie Couric Speckled Malt Eggs.

Matt Lauer I'm kind of a chocolate fanatic, so I'd be partial to chocolate. One colored egg and Chunky bar would do it for me.

Al Roker Giving props to my Peeps.

Ann Curry A dark chocolate bunny.

Q. What do you love to eat at 4th of July gatherings?

Katie Couric I love corn on the cob, fresh tomatoes, and anything cooked on a grill!

Matt Lauer I love to enjoy a backyard BBQ: Hamburgers, hot dogs, cole slaw, potato salad, corn on the cob, the works.

Al Roker Pulled pork BBQ sandwiches.

Ann Curry Fresh corn with real butter and potato salad.

Q. Where do you like to watch the fireworks?

Katie Couric Any place I'm with family and friends and hopefully there's a live orchestra.

Matt Lauer We have a house at the beach, so we go where it's not too crowded, sit on a blanket, enjoy a glass of wine while watching the show over the ocean.

Al Roker From my backyard in upstate New York.

Ann Curry On TV from bed.

Q. What was the best Halloween costume you ever had?

Katie Couric I was Cousin It in the third grade, complete with long strips of brown crepe paper over my face.

Matt Lauer I'd have to say when I dressed up as J. Lo and Al was P Diddy on the show, I don't think I could have topped that as a kid.

Al Roker The Mummy!

Ann Curry Statue of Liberty.

Q. Your favorite Halloween candy is...

Katie Couric Reeses Peanut Butter Cups and Milk Duds (full size please)

Matt Lauer Smarties.

Al Roker Payday Bar.

Ann Curry Snickers.

new year's day
breakfast *hosted by B. Smith*

menu

> Champagne Campari Cocktail > Potato Leek Pancakes
> Salmon Scrambled Eggs

Champagne Campari Cocktail

1   sugar cube, optional
¼   ounce Campari
5   ounces Champagne
    Raspberry for garnish
    Lemon peel for garnish

PLACE sugar cube in a stemmed Champagne flute and pour the Campari over the cube.

FILL slowly with the Champagne. Garnish with lemon peel and raspberry. **serves 1**

Chef Tip: Add a splash of orange juice for a Champagne Campari Mimosa. Substitute Prosecco or a nonalcoholic sparkling wine for the Champagne.

> Potato Leek Pancakes

2 cups grated peeled Idaho
  or russet potatoes
1½ cups finely chopped leeks,
  white part only
2 large eggs, beaten
¼ cup all-purpose flour
1 teaspoon salt
¼ teaspoon ground black pepper
  Vegetable oil
  Salad greens, for serving
  Smoked salmon, crème
  fraîche and caviar, or chunky
  applesauce, for garnish
  Chopped chives, garnish

MIX the potatoes, leeks, eggs, flour, salt, and pepper together in a large bowl until thoroughly combined.

HEAT just enough oil to cover the bottom of a medium-size skillet.

SPOON one-eighth of the mixture into the center of the skillet and spread it out slightly to form a 3-inch circle. Cook over medium heat until golden on the underside. Using a large metal spatula, turn it over and cook until golden on the

other side and cooked through. Repeat with remaining mixture, keeping cooked pancakes warm in the oven.

SERVE warm with smoked salmon, crème fraîche and caviar, or with chunky applesauce. **makes eight 3- to 5-inch or four 6- to 8-inch pancakes**

Chef Tip: The starch in Idaho or russet potatoes helps hold the pancake together. Place grated potatoes on a paper towel and squeeze out excess moisture.

Salmon Scrambled Eggs ◄

8 eggs
3 tablespoons heavy cream
4 tablespoons butter
¾ cup minced smoked salmon
Salt and freshly ground
black pepper
Chopped chives for garnish

CRACK the eggs into bowl and beat them just until the yolks and whites are combined. Add the cream and whisk until the eggs look foamy and light.

HEAT a large non-stick skillet over medium heat for about a minute. Add the butter; swirl it around the pan until it foams.

TURN the heat down to medium low. Cook egg mixture in skillet, stirring frequently, scraping the bottom and sides of the pan until the eggs have thickened into soft, creamy curds, about 10 to 15 minutes.

KEEP stirring, breaking up the curds as you sprinkle in the salmon. Season the eggs with salt and pepper.

TRANSFER to a warm platter while the eggs are slightly underdone. Garnish with chopped chives.

serves 4

Chef Tip: Freshly laid eggs from free-range chickens have deeper colored yolks and are more flavorful.

valentine's day
sweetheart *dinner*

hosted by *the Scotto Family*

menu

> Italian Wedding Soup
> Steak Pizzaiola *with Sun Dried Tomato Polenta*
> Grilled Pizza Margherita > Blood Orange Panna Cotta

Italian Wedding Soup ◄

Meatballs:
- 1 pound ground beef
- 1 cup dried bread crumbs (store-bought are fine)
- 1 egg
- 2 tablespoons chopped fresh parsley
- ½ cup grated Parmesan cheese
- 1 teaspoon kosher salt
- 2 tablespoons cold water

Soup:
- ½ cup olive oil
- 1 cup dried onions
- 2 tablespoons chopped garlic
- 1 tablespoon crushed red pepper flakes
- 2 quarts chicken stock
- 1 cup diced carrots
- 1 cup diced celery
- ½ cup diced zucchini
- 1 pound escarole, chopped
- 5 tablespoons grated Parmesan cheese
- Salt

TO make the meatballs: Place the ground beef in a large bowl.

ADD the bread crumbs, egg, parsley, cheese, salt, and pepper.

WITH wet, cold hands mix the ingredients together well.

ADD the cold water. Form the mixture into about 18 one-inch meatballs. Set aside.

TO make the soup: In a large stockpot, heat the olive oil over medium heat and sauté the onions until they are translucent. Add the garlic and red pepper flakes and sauté for about 5 minutes, or until the onions are glazed.

ADD the chicken stock and bring the soup to a boil over high heat. Add the carrots, celery, onions, and zucchini, lower the heat, and simmer for about 1½ hours, or until the vegetables are tender.

ADD the meatballs and escarole and simmer for 20 minutes. Stir in the cheese and season to taste with salt. Serve warm. **serves 6**

Chef Tip: Always make sure you have plenty of cold water to roll the meatballs.

>Steak Pizzaiola
with sun-dried tomato polenta

2½ pounds beef tenderloin
½ cup olive oil
3 cloves garlic, chopped
1 pound sliced mushrooms
1 can (32 ounces) Italian plum
  tomatoes, optional
¼ cup chopped parsley
1 teaspoon oregano
  Salt and pepper to taste

Sun-Dried Tomato Polenta:
3 cups milk
1 cup water
1 cup instant white polenta
½ cup mascarpone
1 tablespoon chopped garlic
2 tablespoons chopped shallots
½ cup extra-virgin olive oil
½ cup sun-dried tomatoes

PAN sear beef tenderloin over medium heat for 2 to 3 minutes. Remove from sauté pan and set aside.

ADD garlic and mushrooms to pan and sauté for 2 to 3 minutes or until golden brown.

ADD tomatoes, parsley, oregano, and beef tenderloin to sauté pan and simmer over low heat for about 20 minutes. Season with salt and pepper to taste.

TO make the polenta, heat the milk and water in a large pot and bring to a boil. While it is simmering, slowly add the polenta. Stir constantly for 6 to 7 minutes, or until the liquid has been absorbed.

REMOVE from heat and stir in the mascarpone. Set the polenta aside. Next prepare the sun-dried tomatoes. Sauté garlic and shallots in olive oil over low to medium heat until golden brown.

ADD sun-dried tomatoes and cook for about 3 to 5 minutes until soft. Set aside.

PUREE half of sun-dried tomatoes in a blender. The other half should be chopped.

TO finish, combine polenta, chopped sun-dried tomatoes, and puree. Serve immediately. **serves 8 to 10**

Chef Tip: Steak Pizzaiola can be made in advance, but the Sun-Dried Tomato Polenta needs to be prepared just before serving.

Grilled Pizza Margherita ◄

1 quart lukewarm water
1 teaspoon fresh yeast
1 tablespoon molasses
2½ tablespoons kosher salt
1 cup olive oil
3 cups all-purpose flour
3 cups high-gluten flour
½ cup whole-wheat flour
1 cup grated Pecorino
   Romano cheese
1 cup grated Bel Paese cheese
1 cup tomato sauce
3 tablespoons chopped
   fresh parsley
½ cup chopped fresh basil

IN a mixing bowl, combine the water, yeast, and molasses. Mix together gently until all the yeast dissolves. Set the mixture aside for 5 to 10 minutes until the yeast makes a raft. Stir in the salt and olive oil.

WITH the mixer on a low speed, add the three kinds of flour. Mix until all the flour is absorbed and the dough pulls away from the side of the bowl. Roll the dough into one large ball and let it stand for 5 minutes.

CUT the dough into 12 pieces. Roll the pieces into balls and place them on an oiled baking sheet. Brush the balls lightly with olive oil and cover with plastic wrap.

IF you are going to use the dough right away, let it sit at room temperature for 30 minutes before baking. If you don't need the dough immediately, you can store it for one day in the refrigerator, but you must let it sit at room temperature for 1 hour before using.

IN a bowl, combine the cheeses. When the dough is ready, prepare the fire, preferably a charcoal fire, but a gas grill works nicely too. Make sure the grill grid is set at least 4 inches from the fire.

ON an oiled surface, push a piece of dough out using the palms of your hands. If the dough is sticking to the surface, lift it and drizzle a little more oil on the surface. You want the dough to be a 12-inch circle with an even thickness. The shape of the pizza is not as important as the thickness of the dough.

GENTLY lift the dough and, being careful not to tear it, drape it onto the hot spot of the grill. The dough will start to rise immediately. Carefully lift the edge of the dough to see the color of the underside,

which should be evenly golden brown (this should take about 2 minutes).

FLIP the dough over and place it on the side of the grill or a cooler spot of the grill. Brush the cooked side of the dough with olive oil. Take ⅙ of the cheese and evenly spread it out to the very edge of the dough. Next, with a tablespoon, dollop tomato sauce on the pizza (8 to 10 spoonfuls); you don't want to spread the sauce over the whole surface of the pizza. Drizzle the pizza with 1 tablespoon of extra-virgin olive oil and sprinkle with ½ tablespoon of chopped parsley.

CAREFULLY slide the pizza back to the edge of the hot section of the grill and rotate the pizza until the bottom is evenly golden brown. This should take 3 to 4 minutes. Do not put the pizza directly over the fire, because the bottom will burn before the cheese melts. Garnish with the chopped basil and serve immediately. **serves 2 to 4**

Chef Tip: If you like, roll out the dough and cut into heart shapes.

Blood Orange ❮
Panna Cotta

Caramel:
- ½ teaspoon lemon juice
- ½ cup granulated sugar
- 2 tablespoons hot water

Cream:
- 2 envelopes unflavored gelatin
- 2 cups blood orange juice
- 4 cups heavy cream
- 1 cup sugar

MAKE Caramel: Put lemon juice and ½ cup sugar into heavy pot. Cook over high heat, swirling often, until sugar caramelizes. Add hot water "careful" ... caramel will splatter and is very hot. Pour caramel into the bottom of mold.

MAKE Cream: Sprinkle gelatin over orange juice in a small saucepan; set aside to soften.

COMBINE cream and sugar in another saucepan and heat just to dissolve sugar.

HEAT orange juice and gelatin gently to melt gelatin.

COMBINE orange juice mixture and cream mixture. Pour into prepared mold and refrigerate overnight.

TO remove mold, invert onto serving platter just before serving. **serves 6**

Chef Tip: This dessert can stay refrigerated in the mold for up to 3 days. When ready to serve, invert onto serving platter.

celebrate spring
brunch

hosted by **Donata Maggipinto**

menu
> Spring Soup > Baked Ham
> Dried Cherry-Rhubarb Relish > Angel Food Cake

Spring Soup ◀

¾ cup (1½ sticks) unsalted butter
2 tablespoons olive oil
3 medium leeks, well rinsed and coarsely chopped
1 large yellow onion, chopped
3 cloves garlic, minced
8 cups chicken stock or canned chicken broth
2 red potatoes, peeled and diced
2 large bunches broccoli (about 3 pounds total weight), trimmed and stems and florets coarsely chopped
1¼ cups freshly grated Parmesan cheese
½ cup chopped fresh Italian flat-leaf parsley
⅛ teaspoon red pepper flakes
Salt and freshly ground pepper, to taste
½ to ¾ cup heavy cream
1 large red bell pepper, finely diced

IN a large pot over low heat, melt the butter with the olive oil. Add the leeks, onion, and garlic and cook, stirring occasionally, until the vegetables are very soft, about 15 minutes.

ADD the stock and potatoes, increase the heat to medium, and cook, uncovered, until the potatoes are tender, about 15 minutes. Add the broccoli and cook until tender, about 10 minutes. Remove from the heat and stir in 1 cup of the Parmesan, the parsley, red pepper flakes, and the salt and ground pepper to taste. Let stand for 3 minutes.

WORKING in batches, puree the soup in a food processor or a blender. Return the soup to the pan and whisk in the cream in a slow, steady stream. Rewarm the soup over low heat.

TO serve, ladle the soup into serving bowls. Garnish evenly with the diced red pepper and remaining ¼ cup Parmesan cheese. serves 6 to 8

Chef Tip: This soup is a great make-ahead option because it freezes beautifully.

> Baked Ham

½ fully cooked bone-in or boneless butt end ham, about 6 pounds
2 tablespoons whole cloves
½ cup cranberry or red currant jelly
2 tablespoons Dijon mustard
½ teaspoon coarsely ground pepper

LET the ham stand at room temperature for about 1 hour before baking to ensure even cooking. Preheat the oven to 325°F.

SCORE the outside surface of the ham in a diamond pattern, making crosscuts ½ inch apart, and stud the center of each diamond with a clove.

PLACE the ham, rounded side up, in a large roasting pan. Bake for 30 minutes.

MAKE the glaze: In a small bowl, stir together the cranberry jelly, mustard and pepper.

AFTER 5 minutes remove the ham from the oven and brush half of the glaze over the surface of the ham. Return to the oven and bake, basting every 20 minutes with the remaining glaze until it is used up. The ham will take 12 to 15 minutes per pound and is done when the top is golden brown and glistening and an instant-read thermometer inserted into the thickest part registers 140°F, about 1 hour more.

REMOVE from the oven and transfer the ham to a warmed platter. Let the ham rest for 15 minutes before carving. Serve with the Dried Cherry Rhubarb Relish (recipe on page 179). serves 8 to 10

Chef Tip: Let the ham rest 15 minutes before carving. It will be easier to carve and juicer too.

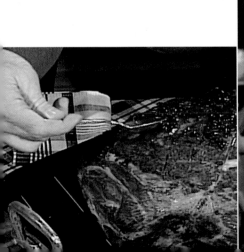

Dried Cherry-Rhubarb Relish

4 cups chopped rhubarb
1 cup dried cherries
1 teaspoon ground cloves
1 teaspoon dry mustard
2 cinnamon sticks
1/2 teaspoon ground allspice
2 tablespoons finely chopped fresh ginger
Grated zest from 1 orange
Grated zest from 1/2 lemon
1/4 cup packed dark brown sugar
2 tablespoons orange juice
1/4 cup balsamic vinegar

IN a large nonreactive saucepan, combine the rhubarb with the remaining ingredients. Bring to a boil, then simmer over low heat until the rhubarb is tender but still maintains it shape, 10 to 12 minutes. Do not stir too often or the rhubarb will begin to disintegrate. Taste for sweetness, adding a bit more brown sugar if needed. Spoon into small jars, cover, and refrigerate up to 3 weeks. Serve at room temperature. makes 2 cups

Chef Tip: This chunky relish, bursting with tart rhubarb, sweet cherries, and pungent spices, is a fitting accompaniment to the baked ham. Be sure to trim off the toxic leaves of the rhubarb before cooking.

Angel Food Cake ◀

1 cup cake flour
1¼ cups superfine sugar
¼ teaspoon salt
1¼ cups egg whites
(from about 10 eggs)
1½ teaspoons cream of tartar
1½ teaspoons vanilla extract
Fresh berries for serving
Confectioners' sugar
for dusting

PREHEAT the oven to 350°F.

SIFT the flour, 1 cup of the superfine sugar, and the salt twice onto a sheet of waxed paper; reserve.

IN the bowl of an electric mixer fitted with the whisk attachment, beat the egg whites on medium speed until foamy. Add the cream of tartar, increase the speed to medium-high and beat until the whites are soft and foamy. Gradually add the remaining ¼ cup superfine sugar and the vanilla extract and beat until medium-firm peaks form when the beaters are lifted. Do not overbeat.

REMOVE the bowl from the mixer. Sift one-fourth of the flour mixture over the egg whites and gently fold in with a rubber spatula. Add the remaining flour mixture in three equal additions, sifting and folding each time.

POUR the batter into a 10-inch ungreased angel food cake pan and gently smooth the top. Bake until the cake is golden and springs back when touched, about 40 minutes. Remove from the oven and invert the pan onto its feet or the neck of a wine bottle. Let cool completely.

GENTLY run a long, thin-bladed knife around the outer sides of the pan, pressing it firmly against the pan to prevent tearing the cake. Then run the knife or a skewer around the inside of the tube. Invert the pan and let the cake slide out. Cut the cake with a serrated knife. Serve with whipped cream and berries.

makes one 10-inch cake

Chef Tip: Eggs are easier to separate when they are cold. If any speck of yolk gets into the whites, the whites will not whip up properly. If a yolk breaks, start fresh with another egg. Let the separated egg whites come to room temperature before using them in the batter.

4th of july
picnic *hosted by Ina Garten*

menu
> Fresh Corn Salad > Grilled Salmon Salad
> Fresh Lemonade > Coconut Cupcakes *with Cream Cheese Icing*

Fresh Corn Salad ◀

5   ears corn, shucked
½   cup small-diced red onion
        (1 small onion)
3   tablespoons cider vinegar
3   tablespoons good olive oil
½   teaspoon kosher salt
½   teaspoon freshly ground
        black pepper
½   cup chiffonade fresh basil leaves

IN a large pot of boiling salted water, cook the corn for 3 minutes until the starchiness is just gone. Drain and immerse it in ice water to stop the cooking and to set the color. When the corn is cool, cut the kernels off the cob, cutting close to the cob.

TOSS the kernels in a large bowl with the red onions, vinegar, olive oil, salt, and pepper. Just before serving, toss in the fresh basil. Taste for seasonings and serve cold or at room temperature. serves 4 to 6

Chef Tip: Don't substitute frozen corn; it doesn't have the texture or flavor you want in a fresh salad.

>Grilled Salmon Salad

2 pounds fresh salmon fillets,
  with the skin on
  Good olive oil, for grilling
  Kosher salt
  Freshly ground black pepper
1 cup small-diced celery
  (3 stalks)
½ cup small-diced red onion
  (1 small onion)
2 tablespoons minced fresh dill
2 tablespoons capers, drained
2 tablespoons raspberry vinegar
2 tablespoons good olive oil
½ teaspoon kosher salt
½ teaspoon freshly ground
  black pepper

PREPARE the grill with hot coals.

CUT the salmon fillets crosswise into 4-inch-wide slices. Rub them with olive oil and sprinkle with salt and pepper. Brush the cooking surface with oil to prevent the fish from sticking. Cook the fillets on the grill for 5 to 7 minutes on each side, until they are rare. Be sure they are still rare on the inside. Remove to a plate, wrap with plastic, and chill in the refrigerator until cold and very firm.

WHEN the fillets are cold, remove any skin that hasn't come off during grilling. Break the fillets into very large flakes and put them into a bowl, adding any juice that has collected at the bottom of the plate.

ADD the celery, red onions, dill, capers, raspberry vinegar, olive oil, salt, and pepper to taste. Mix well and serve cold or at room temperature. serves 4

Chef Tip: Toss all the ingredients together and get the same delicious flavor with less work and fewer bowls.

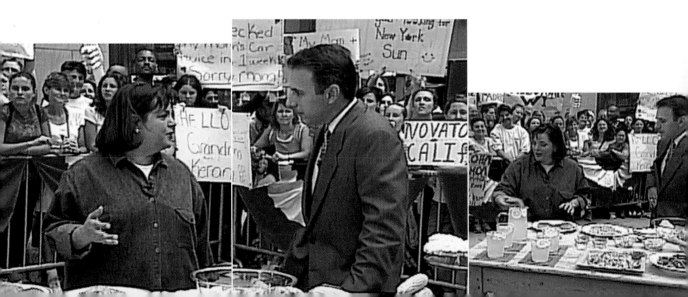

Fresh Lemonade <

1 cup freshly squeezed
   lemon juice (5 to 6 lemons)
½ to ¾ cup superfine sugar,
   to taste
1 cup crushed ice
4 cups water

PLACE all the ingredients in a blender and process until completely smooth. Serve over ice. makes 1½ quarts

Chef Tip: Add a few slices of lemon to the pitcher, or you can just toss in a few squeezed lemon halves.

Coconut Cupcakes ◄
with cream cheese icing

For cupcakes:
- ¾ pound unsalted butter at room temperature
- 2 cups sugar
- 5 extra-large eggs at room temperature
- 1½ teaspoons pure vanilla extract
- 1½ teaspoons pure almond extract
- 3 cups all-purpose flour
- 1 teaspoon baking powder
- ½ teaspoon baking soda
- ½ teaspoon salt
- 1 cup buttermilk
- 14 ounces sweetened, shredded coconut
- Cream Cheese Icing (recipe follows)

For Cream Cheese Icing
- 1 pound cream cheese at room temperature
- ¾ pound unsalted butter at room temperature
- 1 teaspoon pure vanilla extract
- ½ teaspoon pure almond extract
- 1½ pounds confectioners' sugar, sifted

PREHEAT the oven to 325 degrees.

IN the bowl of an electric mixer fitted with a paddle attachment, cream the butter and sugar until light and fluffy, about 5 minutes. With the mixer running on low, add the eggs one at a time, scraping down the bowl after each addition. Add the vanilla and almond extracts and mix well.

IN a separate bowl, sift together the flour, baking powder, baking soda, and salt. In three parts, alternately add the dry ingredients and the buttermilk to the batter, beginning and ending with the dry. Mix until just combined. Fold in 7 ounces of coconut.

LINE a muffin pan with paper liners. Fill each cup to the top with batter. Bake for 25 to 35 minutes, until the tops are brown and a toothpick comes out clean. Allow to cool in the pan for 15 minutes. Remove to a baking rack and cool completely. Frost with cream cheese icing and sprinkle with the remaining coconut.

FOR Cream Cheese Icing: In the bowl of an electric mixer fitted with a paddle attachment, blend together the cream cheese, butter, and vanilla and almond extracts. Add the confectioner' sugar and mix until smooth. makes 18 to 20 large cupcakes

Chef Tip: Use an ice cream scoop to fill the muffin cups.

halloween
spook-tacular
party *hosted by* Sandra Lee

menu

> Southwestern Turkey Chili *with Corn Bread*
> Finger Sandwiches > Black Cat and Bat Parfaits
> Creepy Crunchy Donut Eyeballs

Southwestern Turkey
Chili *with corn bread*

Corn Bread
Nonstick vegetable cooking
spray, Pam®
1 can (11-ounce) Mexicorn,
Green Giant®
1 egg
1 package (8½-ounce) corn
muffin mix, Jiffy®

Chili
10 ounces lean ground turkey,
crumbled
1 tablespoon all-purpose flour,
Pillsbury®
1 tablespoon olive oil, Bertolli®
1 can (15.5-ounce) spicy black
beans, S&W Regional Recipe:
San Antonio Beans®
1 can (14½-ounce) stewed
tomatoes, Mexican recipe
style, S&W®
Garnishes: sour cream,
chopped fresh cilantro,
chopped red onion

PREHEAT oven to 400°F.

SPRAY 8×8×2-inch baking pan with nonstick spray. Drain all but 2 tablespoons liquid from Mexicorn. Place reserved 2 tablespoons liquid in a medium bowl. Add egg to liquid and whisk to blend. Stir in Mexicorn. Add corn muffin mix and stir until just blended. Transfer mixture to prepared pan. Bake until a toothpick inserted into center of corn bread comes out clean, about 20 minutes.

IN a zip-top bag, toss turkey with flour, until flour is absorbed into meat. Heat oil in a wide 2-quart pot over medium heat. Sauté the turkey until browned, about 5 minutes. Add the beans and tomatoes. Simmer over medium-low heat until chili is slightly thick, about 8 minutes. Spoon chili into bowls. Top with sour cream, cilantro, and onion. Serve hot with corn bread. serves 2

Chef Tip: Cover tightly and store leftover corn bread at room temperature for up to 3 days. Cover tightly and store leftover chili in refrigerator for up to 3 days. Reheat over medium heat.

>Finger Sandwiches

MAKE sandwiches on white bread using pimiento cheese, chicken salad, ham, turkey, or roast beef. Trim the crusts from sandwiches and cut into long, narrow "fingers." Carve a slice of tomato skin into a fingernail and attach it with mayonnaise.

PLACE cuts at the bottom of the "finger" sandwich with a serrated blade that's been smeared with red food coloring.

Chef Tip: Arrange these "fingers" on a black plate. Use orange fabric for a table covering and continue the theme with orange and black napkins and plastic utensils.

Black Cat and Bat Parfaits

1 box (3-ounce) orange gelatin, Jell-O®
20 chocolate sandwich cookies, Nabisco®
3 cups whipped topping, thawed, Cool Whip®
4 individual, ready-to-eat butterscotch puddings, Kraft®
½ cup caramel sauce, Mrs. Richardson's®

PREPARE gelatin according to box instructions. Divide equally among 4 parfait or tall glasses.

REFRIGERATE until set. Place cookies in a zip-lock plastic storage bag and crush with a rolling pin. Divide crushed cookies in half. Sprinkle one half of the crushed cookies over set gelatin in each glass. Top the crushed cookies with ¼ cup of whipped topping. Sprinkle second half of the crushed cookies over whipped topping. Spoon butterscotch pudding (one for each parfait) into glasses, then divide remaining whipped topping between four glasses. Swirl into a peak. Drizzle with caramel sauce before serving. serves 4

Chef Tip: Garnish the parfaits with assorted Halloween candies. Look for candies shaped like cats, bats, spiders, and other creepy things.

Creepy Crunchy ‹
Donut Eyeballs

2 bags (12 ounce) white
   chocolate morsels, Nestlé®
4 teaspoons vegetable
   shortening, Crisco®
20 glazed donut holes,
   Entenmann's®
20 round jellied candies,
   Gummi Savers®
20 milk chocolate candies, M&M's®
   Red food coloring, Schilling®

LINE a cookie sheet with parchment paper or wax paper and set aside. Melt chocolate morsels with vegetable shortening in a stainless steel bowl by setting bowl over a pan of simmering water and stirring until smooth. Cut two $\frac{1}{8}$-inch slices from opposite sides of each donut hole.

DROP the donut holes into the chocolate, one at a time. Using a fork, coat the donut hole in chocolate. Lift and gently shake to remove excess chocolate. Place on prepared cookie sheet, cut side down. Repeat with remaining donut holes. Reserve unused chocolate. Place the jellied candies on top surface of donut holes. Refrigerate until set. Re-heat chocolate if necessary. Place a small dab of melted chocolate on the chocolate candies and stick them onto the jellied candies.

REFRIGERATE until set, about 10 minutes. In a small bowl, mix 2 drops of food coloring with 2 teaspoons melted chocolate. Use a toothpick to draw "veins" on the eyeballs. Refrigerate until ready to serve. serves 20

Chef Tip: Send some of these to school with your little goblins. They're frightfully good fun for the office too.

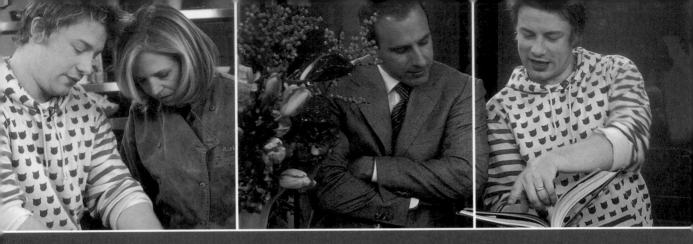

thanksgiving
feast *hosted by* Jamie Oliver

menu

> Mozzarella and Butternut Squash Skewers
> Jamie's Thanksgiving Stuffing
> Roast Turkey > Apple Pie

Mozzarella and Butternut ◄ Squash Skewers

1 butternut squash
1 teaspoon dried chili, crushed
1 tablespoon coriander seeds,
   crushed
   Nutmeg, finely grated
   Dried oregano
   Salt and freshly ground
   black pepper
   Olive oil
3 balls of buffalo mozzarella
   Wooden skewers, 4 inches
1 fresh red chili, 4 inches, chopped
   Few leaves of basil

PREHEAT your oven to 400°F. Chop the squash in half and scoop out the seeds with a teaspoon. Slice each half into 4 parts lengthways and place in a bowl. Sprinkle with the chili, coriander, nutmeg, oregano, and a little salt and freshly ground black pepper. Toss with a splash of oil, place on a roasting tray, and then roast in the preheated oven for 40 minutes or until softened, cooked through, and lightly browned.

CAREFULLY cut the squash into large cubes, and tear the mozzarella up into similar-sized pieces. Make a skewer with a piece of chili, a basil leaf folded in half, a piece of mozzarella, and a chunk of squash. Repeat until all the bits of squash and mozzarella are used up, and drizzle with olive oil before serving.

makes a few servings

>Jamie's Thanksgiving Stuffing

2 celery sticks, finely chopped
4 shallots, finely chopped
Small handful of fresh sage, finely chopped
6 strips pancetta, finely chopped
2 ounces butter
Big handful of fresh bread crumbs (bread stuffing), coarsely chopped
Handful dried apricots, coarsely chopped
Salt and freshly ground black pepper
5 or 6 chestnuts (roasted or jarred), coarsely chopped
¾ pound freshly ground pork
Pinch of grated nutmeg
1 egg

FINELY chop the celery, shallots, sage, and pancetta and add with butter to a hot frying/sauté pan. Fry gently on medium heat until everything is lightly golden brown. Take off the heat.

TO prepare the fresh bread crumbs, take a loaf of day-old bread, remove the crust, and place the chunks of bread in a food processor until the bread is coarsely chopped. Add the bread crumbs and coarsely chopped apricots and chestnuts to the celery, shallots, sage, pancetta, and butter mixture. Season well to taste with salt and pepper. Mix well and chill.

WHEN the stuffing is cold, add the pork, nutmeg, and egg. Refrigerate until ready to use. makes enough for a 9- to 10-pound turkey

Chef Tip: You can make the stuffing a day or two in advance to help lighten the load on Thanksgiving Day.

Roast Turkey ◄

9 to 10-pound organic
   free-range turkey
   Salt and freshly ground black
   pepper
4 shallots, roughly chopped
   At least 8 cloves of garlic,
   2 peeled
2 carrots
6 strips pancetta (smoked
   bacon), sliced in half
12 small fresh rosemary sprigs,
   plus a few extra
1 big orange
   Olive oil
1 teaspoon flour
   A little white wine or sherry
   (optional)
1 quart vegetable stock,
   for the gravy

PREHEAT the oven to 350ºF. To prep the turkey, rub it with salt, inside and out, 12 to 24 hours before cooking; table salt is fine. Store the salted turkey in a plastic bag and refrigerate. When ready to cook, rinse or wipe off excess salt. Pat it dry with paper towels and place on a board. Make a bed of roughly chopped shallots, 6 unpeeled garlic cloves, and carrots in your roasting pan to act as a rack.

SLICE the strips of pancetta in half and slice the peeled garlic into thin slivers. Place a rosemary sprig and a garlic sliver on one end of a strip of pancetta and roll it up tightly. Repeat with the other pieces of pancetta until you have 12 little rolls.

STAB the thighs and drumsticks of the turkey in 6 places on each side. Push your finger into each slit to create a gap. Place each pancetta roll into the holes until it just peeps out. Find the edge of the skin at the turkey neck and with a rubber spatula or large spoon separate the skin from breast meat so that you can put the stuffing under the skin of the turkey breast. If you're careful you should be able to separate all the skin from the meat, keeping it attached at the sides but without ripping any holes in it.

FROM the neck end of the turkey, spoon the stuffing up between the skin and the breast, tucking the flap of skin underneath to stop any leaking out during cooking. Microwave the orange for 30 to 60 seconds to get it nice and hot. Poke a hole in the hot orange and stuff it into the turkey cavity. You can also add some rosemary to the cavity.

PLACE the bird in roasting pan filled with the vegetables, season well with salt and pepper, and rub olive oil all over. Weigh the stuffed bird, cover with foil, and roast for 18 minutes per pound, or until the juices run clear from the thigh if pierced with a knife or a skewer. Remove foil for the last 45 minutes to brown the bird.

REMOVE the turkey and rest on a board for 20 minutes.

REMOVE most of the fat from the roasting pan. Mash the roast vegetables right in the pan with a potato masher. Add the flour, sherry, and stock and bring to a boil on a high heat. When the gravy thickens, strain into a bowl. Serve the turkey with the gravy.

serves 6 to 8

Chef Tip: I push sage and apricot stuffing up under the turkey breast skin, increasing the thickness of the breasts so they take the same time to cook as the legs. The result? Juicy turkey all 'round!

Apple Pie ◀

For the pastry:
- 2 cups flour
- 10 tablespoons butter
- 2½ tablespoons sugar
- Finely grated rind of 1 lemon
- 2 egg yolks

For the filling:
- A small knob of butter
- Flour, for dusting
- 1 large Bramley or other cooking apple
- 4 eating apples (try Cox's or Braeburn)
- 3 tablespoons Demerara or brown sugar
- Zest of ½ a lemon
- ½ teaspoon ground ginger
- A handful of sultanas or raisins
- 1 egg yolk mixed with a splash of milk

PREHEAT the oven to 300°F. To make the pastry, in a food processor, whizz up the flour, butter, sugar, and lemon rind, then add the egg yolks and a tiny drop of water to bind the mix together. Butter an 8 inch metal pie dish—use a metal one because it will conduct heat better so the bottom of the pie will cook at the same time as the top.

DIVIDE your pastry dough into two and roll half of it out on a flour-dusted surface until ¼ inch thick. Lay the pastry in the pie dish and gently push it down into the sides. Don't worry if it tears or breaks— just patch it up—as it will look nice and rustic! Pop the pie dish and the remaining half of your pastry into the fridge while you peel your apples. Quarter the cooking apple and cut the eating apples into eighths. Toss the apples in a small pan with the sugar, lemon zest, ginger, sultanas or raisins, and a tablespoon of water. Simmer gently for 5 minutes or until the apples are just tender. Remove from the heat and allow to cool completely.

REMOVE the pie dish and pastry from the fridge and pack the apple mix tightly into the pie dish. Egg-wash the pastry rim and then roll out the other half of the dough. Drape this over the top of the pie and roughly pinch the edges together using your finger and thumb and trim any excess pastry. Egg-wash the top, make a couple of small incisions and bake for 45 to 50 minutes. Spoon out the portions of apple pie and serve with some custard! serves 6

holiday dinner
italian-style
hosted by **Sal Scognamillo**

menu
> Baccala Salad > Seasoned Bread Crumb Shrimp Scampi
> Frank Sinatra's Veal Cutlets Milanese > Zeppoles

Baccala Salad ◀

2 pounds skinless, boneless salt cod (baccala)
¼ cup olive oil
Juice of two lemons
20 gaeta olives, pits removed
1 garlic clove, minced
2 tablespoons finely minced fresh basil
Salt and freshly ground black pepper, to taste

IN refrigerator, soak cod in several changes of cold water for 4 to 5 days. (Baccala—salt cod—is available in many supermarkets and specialty stores.) Remove cod from the soaking water and cut into 3-inch pieces. Place in a large saucepan, cover with water and bring to a boil. Reduce flame to medium and cook until fish flakes easily, about 15 to 20 minutes. Drain and place cod in cold water to cool for 10 to 15 minutes. Meanwhile, make a marinade by combining the oil, lemon juice, gaeta olives (available in specialty stores), garlic and basil in a large bowl. Season to taste with salt and pepper. Flake the cooled cod with a fork and add to the vinaigrette, mixing gently to coat thoroughly. Refrigerate for at least 1 hour, to infuse the flavors. Serve chilled or at room temperature.

serves 6

Chef Tip: Keep pouring the marinade over the cod to infuse all of the flavors.

> ## Seasoned Bread Crumb Shrimp Scampi

Shrimp Scampi

- 4 tablespoons unsalted butter
- 8 garlic cloves, minced
- 16 jumbo shrimp (about 1½ pounds), peeled and deveined
  Juice of 2 lemons
- ¼ cup clam juice or broth
  Dash of Worcestershire sauce
- ½ teaspoon paprika
- ½ cup Seasoned Bread Crumbs
- 2 tablespoons olive oil
  Salt and freshly ground black pepper, to taste

Seasoned Bread Crumbs

- ½ small Italian-style baguette, stale (about ½ pound)
- 3 tablespoons freshly grated Parmigiano-Reggiano cheese
- ¼ cup minced flat-leaf parsley
  Pinch of oregano
- 1 garlic clove, minced
- 3 tablespoons olive oil
  Salt and freshly ground black pepper, to taste

PREHEAT the broiler.

HEAT the butter in an ovenproof skillet over low flame and sauté the garlic until lightly golden, about 2 to 3 minutes. Add the shrimp and continue to cook for 1 to 2 minutes, or until the shrimp are coated with the garlic butter. Add the lemon juice, clam juice and Worcestershire sauce, and bring to a boil. Cover, reduce the heat to low and simmer for 1 to 2 minutes.

UNCOVER the skillet, sprinkle the shrimp with the paprika and place under the broiler for 5 to 6 minutes, or until the shrimp are lightly browned and cooked through. Remove the skillet, top the mixture with the bread crumbs, drizzle with the oil and return to the broiler for 2 minutes, or until the bread crumbs are lightly browned. **serves 4**

For the Seasoned Bread Crumbs:
BREAK or cut the bread into large chunks and place in a food processor. Process until reduced to fine crumbs. Transfer to a large bowl. Stir in the cheese, parsley, oregano and garlic. Gradually add oil, stirring, until thoroughly combined. Season to taste with salt and pepper. Place in an airtight jar and cover. Refrigerate until needed. Use within 5 days.

Chef Tip: Sauté the shrimp only briefly in the pan. The majority of the cooking should be down under the broiler. This gives the shrimp greater flavor.

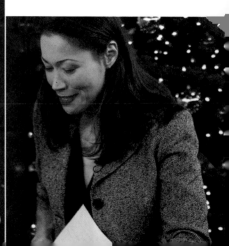

Frank Sinatra's Veal ◄ Cutlets Milanese

½ small Italian stale baguette
    (about ½ pound)
2 tablespoons freshly grated
    Parmigiano-Reggiano
    Pinch of oregano
¼ cup minced flat-leaf parsley
1 cup plus 3 tablespoons olive oil
¼ teaspoon salt
⅛ teaspoon freshly ground
    black pepper
½ cup all-purpose flour
2 large eggs, beaten
8 veal cutlets (about 1¼ pounds),
    pounded thin to slightly less
    than ¼ inch
    Salt and freshly ground black
    pepper to taste
1 lemon, cut into 8 wedges

BREAK or cut the bread into large chunks and place in a food processor. Process until the bread is reduced into fine crumbs. Transfer the crumbs into a large bowl and stir in the cheese, oregano and parsley. Gradually add 3 tablespoons of oil, stirring until thoroughly combined. Season with salt and pepper. Spread the flour onto a large plate, place the eggs in a shallow bowl and spread the seasoned bread crumbs on a second large plate. Coat each veal cutlet in the flour, then the beaten eggs and then the bread crumbs, patting with the palm of your hand to ensure adhesion. Heat 1 cup of the oil in a large nonstick skillet over medium-high flame (to a frying temperature of 350°F.) and sauté the veal for 2 minutes. Turn and sauté for 1 additional minute. Do not crowd the pan. If necessary, fry the cutlets in batches. Remove with a slotted spatula and drain on paper towels. Season to taste with salt and pepper and serve with lemon wedges. serves 8

Chef Tip: When frying the veal cutlets, do not overcrowd the pan. If you overcrowd, the oil cools, causing the cutlets to absorb most of the oil and become greasy.

Zeppoles ◄

2 cups water
1 tablespoon butter
Pinch of salt
2 cups flour
6 eggs
Vegetable oil for frying
2 pounds of ricotta cheese
1½ cups sugar
1 teaspoon vanilla extract
½ cup semisweet chocolate chips
12 maraschino cherries

BRING water, butter, and salt to a boil. When boiling, add flour and stir until thoroughly mixed for about 1 minute. Take off fire. Put into mixing bowl and cool for 10 minutes. Mixing at a medium speed add 1 egg at a time, allowing each egg to blend. Put in a pastry bag. Cut wax paper into 3-inch squares and lightly dust with flour. Pipe into doughnut shapes on squares. Heat oil to 350°F. Carefully slide batter off the wax into the oil. Fry for 7 to 8 minutes turning every couple of minutes. Doughnuts should double in size. Allow to cool. Slice horizontally. Mix ricotta, sugar and vanilla extract in another mixing bowl on medium speed for 2 minutes. Add chocolate chips and mix for 10 seconds. Put cream in pastry bag and fill center of zeppole. Press the top of the pastry onto the bottom. Sprinkle with powdered sugar and place a cherry on top of each pastry. **serves 12**

Chef Tip: You must keep the temperature uniform. If you do not the zeppoles will either burn or undercook.

> Chef & Celebrity Biographies

Curtis G. Aikens

Curtis' career as a television personality and author began in 1988. He resides in Novato, California, and Conyers, Georgia. He is the father of two young sons, Curtis Jr. and Cole. He is a founding member of a new production company, 4 Smart Women and A Dumb Guy. Their first show, *Recipes For Living,* airs in northern California. E-mail Curtis at **www.curtisaikens.com** or at **www.recipesforliving.tv.**

Curtis is the author of *Cooking Is a Family Affair (Recipes from Three Generations of Aikens), Curtis Cooks With Heart and Soul* (Hearst Books), as well as the *Garden Grocer's Guide to the Harvest* and *Curtis Aikens' Guide to the Harvest* (Peachtree Publishers). These popular books combine delicious down-home cooking with Curtis' unique philosophy. He donates a portion of the royalties from these books to literacy programs across the country.

Colman Andrews

Colman Andrews is the editor-in-chief of *SAVEUR* and co-author and co-editor of *Saveur Cooks Authentic American, Saveur Cooks Authentic French,* and *Saveur Cooks Authentic Italian.* He is also author of three acclaimed food books of his own: *Everything on the Table, Flavors of the Riviera,* and *Catalan Cuisine.*

Colman, who has been writing professionally about food, wine, and the arts since 1968, was one of the first 50 American food and wine figures to be named to *Who's Who of Cooking in America.* He is the recipient of the 1996 Bert Greene Award for magazine food journalism and the 1998 M.F.K. Fisher Distinguished Writing award, among other honors. Under his editorship, *SAVEUR* was awarded the 2000 National Magazine Award for General Excellence. He lives in Riverside, Connecticut.

Polka Dot Cheesecake Adapted excerpt from *Maida Heatter's Cakes* (Cader Books/Andrews McMeel, 1997).

Maya Angelou

Maya Angelou, the renowned author, poet and playwright, was born as Marguerite Johnson in St. Louis, Missouri, on April 4, 1928. She attended public schools in Stamps, Arkansas, and San Francisco. Fluent in six languages, Maya has received numerous awards for her inspiring books and plays.

In her cookbook, *Hallelujah! The Welcome Table,* she shares her favorite recipes and accounts of the role food and cooking has played throughout her life.

Recipes from *Hallelujah! The Welcome Table* by Maya Angelou, copyright © 2004 by Maya Angelou. Used by permission of Random House, Inc.

Mario Batali

Mario Batali believes that olive oil is as precious as gold, that shorts are acceptable attire for every season, and food, like most things, is best when left to its own simple beauty. To that end, Mario creates magic night after night in Manhattan's West Village and Theater District, dividing his time among his many Italian hotspots, the flagship of which is Babbo Ristorante e Enoteca, an upscale dining room where Mario has seamlessly combined traditional Italian principles with intelligent culinary adventure since June 1998.

Always eager to educate the masses about the simple beauty that is Italian cuisine, Mario hosts two popular television programs, *Molto Mario* and *Mario Eats Italy,* both on the Food Network. Mario splits his time between New York City's Greenwich Village and Northport, Michigan, with his wife, Susi Cahn of Coach Dairy Goat Farm, and their two sons, Benno and Leo.

Marinated Butternut Squash (Scapece di Zucca; Stuffed Onions (Cipolle Ripiene); Veal Chops Pizzaiolo; Mushroom Fricasse: from *Mario Batali Holiday Food* by Mario Batali. Copyright © 2000 by Mario Batali. Photographs copyright © 2000 by Quentin Bacon. Reprinted by permission of Clarkson Potter, a division of Random House, Inc.

Daniel Boulud

Daniel Boulud, creator of the DANIEL BOULUD KITCHEN line of cookware, is the chef-owner of Manhattan's four-star restaurant DANIEL, renowned for its contemporary, seasonal French cuisine and decor inspired by a Venetian Renaissance palazzo.

Daniel's other award-winning restaurants include Café Boulud and DB Bistro Moderne in New York and a second Café Boulud in Palm Beach, Florida. Daniel Boulud Brasserie opened at the Wynn Resort in Las Vegas in April 2005. After training with some of the most renowned chefs in France, Daniel came to the U.S. from his native Lyon in 1981. He became Chef at the famed Le Cirque, making it one of the country's most acclaimed restaurants before going on to open his own in 1993. Five cookbooks, Feast & Fêtes Catering, and the "DB CONNOISSEUR" line of Caspian caviar and Scottish smoked salmon are some of the chef's other culinary endeavors.

Chicken Satay with Spicy Peanut Sauce; Lamb Stew with Rosemary and Orange: Reprinted from *Daniel's Dish: Entertaining at Home with a Four-Star Chef,* Daniel Boulud, Filipacchi Publishing, 2003.

Rosemary Braised Veal Shank Reprinted from *Chef Daniel Boulud: Cooking in New York City,* Daniel Boulud and Peter Kaminsky, Assouline, 2002.

Short Ribs Braised in Red Wine Reprinted from *Daniel Boulud's Café Boulud Cookbook,* Daniel Boulud and Dorie Greenspan, Scribner, November 1999.

Karen Brooks & Diane Morgan

Karen Brooks, arts and culture editor of *The Oregonian,* has co-authored numerous books, including the best-selling *Atomic Cocktails, Highballs, High Heels, Patio Daddy-O, Dude Food,* and *Dressed to Grill* (all from Chronicle Books). She lives in Portland, Oregon. Read her restaurant reviews at **www.oregonlive.com.**

Diane Morgan, is an experienced cooking teacher, freelance writer, and author of many cookbooks, including *Salmon, The Thanksgiving Table, Dressed to Grill, Delicious Dips,* and *Cooking for the Week* (all from Chronicle Books). She has written for the *Los Angeles Times, Fine Cooking, Bon Appetit,* and *Cooking Light.* She lives in Portland, Oregon. You may visit her website at **www.dianemorgancooks.com.**

Ellen Carroll

Ellen Carroll, M.S., R.D., a Registered Dietitian by training, was a mover and shaker in the healthy eating movement before it was in vogue. As part of the faculty at the

University of Florida, Ellen spent four years teaching nutrition and healthy cooking to professionals and consumers prior to joining *Southern Living* in 1984. There she wrote the *Cooking Light* column for three years before being promoted to the magazine when it launched in 1987.

An accomplished author and editor, Ellen has written more than 300 articles for consumer publications. Her press credits include *Cooking Light, Southern Living,* and *Progressive Farmer* magazines. She is also the editor of seven *Cooking Light* special interest publications.

Ellen is a national television personality, having appeared as a frequent guest on NBC's *Today* show for the past nine years. Her other appearances include Lifetime TV for Women, the Food Network, HGTV, The Discovery Channel, and numerous local and regional stations.

Tom Colicchio

Tom Colicchio, an award-winning chef and author, spent his childhood immersed in food, cooking with his mother and grandmother. However, it was his father who suggested that he make a career of it. Tom taught

himself to cook with the help of Jacques Pépin's illustrated manuals on French cooking, *La Technique* and *La Methode*. At the age of 17, Tom made his kitchen debut in his native town of Elizabeth, New Jersey, at Evelyn's Seafood restaurant.

Tom cooked at various prominent New York restaurants before opening Gramercy Tavern in Manhatten's Gramercy Park neighborhood in 1994. In March 2001, one block south of Gramercy Tavern, Tom opened Craft.

In addition to Gramercy Tavern, Craft, Craftbar, and 'wichcraft in New York City, Tom opened Craftsteak at the MGM Grand in Las Vegas in 2002. With the opening of Craftbar in 2002, Tom introduced his own private label, Craftkitchen, a line of olive oils and condiments he imports from Calabria, Italy. His first cookbook, *Think Like a Chef,* (Clarkson Potter/Publishers, 2000) won a James Beard KitchenAid Cookbook Award. Tom's second cookbook, *Craft of Cooking* (Clarkson Potter/Publishers, 2003), will soon be followed by a sandwich book inspired by 'wichcraft.

Sara & Mary Corpening

Sara Corpening Whiteford and Mary Corpening Barber are twin sisters and the former owners of Thymes Two Catering in San Francisco. Thymes Two has evolved into a culinary consulting and cookbook authoring partnership. Together the sisters have authored *Smoothies, Wraps, Simplify Entertaining, Cocktail Food, Super Smoothies, Skewer It!* and *Bride & Groom First and Forever Cookbook.* They have written numerous articles and recipes for a wide variety of publications, including *Bon Appetit, Food and Wine, American Home Style, Fine Cooking, Cooking Light, Victoria,* and *Health* magazines.

Mary and Sara also do recipe consulting for cutting-edge concepts such as Dlush, a youth beverage joint in San Diego, and Otis, a swank cocktail lounge in San Francisco. For more information, visit their website at **www.thymestwo.com.**

Kathleen Daelemans

Kathleen Daelemans is the author of *Getting Thin and Loving Food.* She was the host of *Cooking Thin with Kathleen Daelemans,* a nationally broadcast weekly show on the Food

Network. Her story and recipes have been featured in *People* and on *The Oprah Winfrey Show.* Her previous book, *Cooking Thin with Chef Kathleen,* was a national bestseller.

Todd English

One of the most decorated, respected, and charismatic chefs in the world, Todd English has enjoyed a staggering amount of accolades during his remarkable career. His accomplishments include recognition by several of the food industry's most prestigious publications, establishing one of the best-known restaurant brands in the nation, and publishing three critically acclaimed cookbooks.

Todd is currently the chef and owner of Olives in Charlestown, Massachusetts. Olives opened in April 1989 as a 50-seat storefront restaurant. It has drawn national and international applause for Todd's interpretive rustic Mediterranean cuisine. Olives now occupies a larger space down the street from its original location in Charlestown. In recent years, Todd has established Olives as one of the most prestigious names in the nation by opening other locations in New York; Las Vegas; Washington, D.C.; Aspen, Colorado;

and Tokyo. He also has four Figs restaurants in the greater Boston area and two locations at LaGuardia Airport in New York City, plus several other well-known restaurants throughout the United States.

Todd has authored the critically acclaimed cookbooks *The Olives Table, The Figs Table,* and *The Olives Dessert Table,* published by Simon & Schuster.

Tyler Florence

Having traveled the globe to help people with their cooking challenges and to introduce them to the kitchens of the world, Chef Tyler Florence has developed a unique perspective on how Americans like to eat and cook today. He has been recognized as a leading chef by publications such as *Bon Appetit, Food & Wine, GQ, Wall Street Journal* and *USA Weekend* and incidentally, was named the Sexiest Chef Alive in 2003 by *People* magazine. Tyler graduated with honors from the College of Culinary Arts at Johnson & Wales University in South Carolina, which recognized his achievements of the last 12 years with an honorary doctorate in spring 2004.

Tyler's debut cookbook, *Tyler Florence's Real Kitchen* (Clarkson

Potter), which hit bookstores nationwide April 2003, was nominated for an IACP award. His second cookbook, *Eat This Book,* was published in April of 2005.

Sara Foster

Sara Foster is one of the country's most beloved and respected experts on simple, honest food prepared with fresh, local, and seasonal ingredients. She is owner and operator of Foster's Market, two gourmet food market cafes in Durham and Chapel Hill, North Carolina.

Sara also is contributing food editor for *Cottage Living* and author of the best-selling *The Foster's Market Cookbook* and *Fresh Every Day: More Great Recipes from Foster's Market.* She has worked alongside Martha Stewart as a chef for Martha's catering company and started her own catering business.

Sara has been featured in the *New York Times, Bon Appetit, Southern Living, Martha Stewart Living Magazine* and has appeared on NBC's *Today* show, *From Martha's Kitchen, Turner South's Home Plate,* and QVC, among others. She also spends several days a month traveling to teach cooking classes and appear as a guest chef at culinary programs for Viking and Williams-Sonoma. Despite this busy schedule, you can still find Sara in the Foster's Market kitchen sharing her love for and pleasure in preparing a home-cooked meal.

Ina Garten

In 1978, Ina Garten left her job as a budget analyst at the White House to pursue her dream: operating a specialty food store in the Hamptons. Owner of the Barefoot Contessa for 20 years, she has written four phenomenally successful cookbooks: *The Barefoot Contessa Cookbook, Barefoot Contessa Parties, Barefoot Contessa Family Style,* and *Barefoot in Paris,* all published by Clarkson Potter. Combined, there are more than 1 million copies of her books in print. Her highly rated Food Network cooking show, *Barefoot Contessa,* premiered in November 2002. Ina and her husband, Jeffrey, divide their time between East Hampton, New York, and Connecticut.

Tanya Holland

Tanya Holland is the author of *New Soul Cooking: Updating a Cuisine Rich in Flavor and Tradition* (Stewart, Tabori & Chang, October 2003) and host of Food Network's *Melting Pot Soul Kitchen* series. Guest appearances include the *Today* show, *The Wayne Brady Show,* and *The Jane Pauley Show.* Holland earned a B.A. in Russian Language from the University of Virginia and a Grande Diplôme from La Varenne Ecole de Cuisine in France.

Tanya cooked at Oyster Bar and L'Etoile on Martha's Vineyard, Hamersley's Bistro in Boston, and Mesa Grill and Verbena Restaurants in New York City before receiving rave reviews as the Executive Chef of The Delux Cafe in Boston and The Victory Kitchen in Brooklyn. Holland has been featured in *Food & Wine, The Wall Street Journal, Savoy,* and the *San Francisco Chronicle.*

Nigella Lawson

Nigella Lawson is a best-selling cookbook author, television personality, and "domestic goddess." An Oxford-educated British journalist, Nigella turns out lively books including *How to Eat, How to Be a Domestic Goddess, Nigella Bites,* and *Forever Summer.* She demonstrates a casual yet sophisticated approach to living in her TV shows—*Nigella Bites* cooking show on the Style Network and E! Entertainment Television and *Forever Summer with Nigella* on Style Network. With Sebastian Conran, she has designed The Living Kitchen collection of housewares. Nigella is the widowed mother of two children, ages 8 (Bruno) and 10 (Mimi), and has a stepchild, Phoebe, who is 9 years old.

Sandra Lee

Sandra Lee is the internationally acclaimed lifestylist, *New York Times* bestselling author, and CEO of Sandra Lee Semi-Homemade® Inc.—a multimedia enterprise focusing on quick and easy solutions for everyday living conveyed through television, books, magazines, and branded products.

Sandra created and patented one of the highest-selling home decorating lines ever invented. This incredible success led Sandra to expand her vision into gardening, craft, and cooking categories.

Sandra Lee's first cookbook, *Semi-Homemade® Cooking*, was released in 2002 and quickly became a *New York Times* best seller. Her next book, *Semi Homemade® Desserts*, was also a sweet success. Semi-Homemade® is based on Sandra's ingenious 70/30 philosophy— 70 percent store-bought/ready-made products accompanied by 30 percent fresh and creative touches.

Sandra demonstrates her unique ideas in her TV show, *Semi-Homemade® Cooking with Sandra Lee* on the Food Network. She has become the expert whom time-starved, overextended homemakers turn to for help.

Donata Maggipinto

A nationally known entertaining and home-style expert, and the lifestyle contributor for NBC's *Today* show, Donata Maggipinto inspires people to celebrate every day in simple ways. With her abundant creativity, relaxed style, and real-life approach, as evidenced in her numerous books, articles, and television appearances, Donata is a leading authority for living happily at home today.

Discover Donata's wisdom and sense of fun, along with her ideas, tips, and guidance for savoring life at home, in her books: *Everyday Celebrations, Christmas Family Gatherings,* and *Halloween Treats.* Donata lives in Marin County, California, with her husband, sons, miniature dachshund, Carolina dog, and tabby cat.

Debbie Martell

Tony Martell, Chairman and Founder of the T.J. Martell Foundation, lost his son T.J. to leukemia in 1975. T.J.'s sister Debbie, the Martells' only daughter, is a nutritionist and chef.

She is a graduate of The Culinary Institute of New York and earned a degree in Nutrition and Dietetics from Arizona State University. Formerly a New York City resident, Debbie worked at such notable restaurants as Union Square Cafe, An American Place and Gotham Bar & Grill.

She now works in Tempe, Arizona, at Athletes' Performance, a facility dedicated to improving the skills of amateur and professional athletes. Some of the training programs include baseball, basketball, football, golf, tennis, and soccer. Debbie is a "performance chef" applying her skills to further the nutritional needs of these athletes. She designs her meals within nutritional guidelines, timing of meals, quality of ingredients, and taste.

Some of Debbie's clients include Jennifer Capriati, Curt Schilling, Nomar Garciaparra, and Mia Hamm.

Nobuyuki Matsuhisa

Nobuyuki Matsuhisa—known to the world simply as "Nobu"—is the acclaimed and highly influential chef-proprietor of Nobu and Matsuhisa restaurants all over the globe, from Beverly Hills to New York City, London to Tokyo, Miami Beach to Las Vegas, Aspen to Milan.

He was named one of "America's 10 Best New Chefs." The Zagat Guide called Nobu "the man who may be the best Japanese chef in the world, creating dishes that have no equal in a cooking style that's part Peruvian and part Nobu's alone." Dishes like squid pasta with light garlic sauce, sashimi salad, silken seared cod, tiger shrimp, and grilled salmon were praised for their ingenuity and unconventional excellence. Zagat named Matsuhisa one of the most popular spots in L.A., "offering the best sushi outside of Japan and seafood dishes like we've never tasted anywhere else; hauntingly good food that is absolutely world-class."

Cary Neff

Trained in classic French kitchens, Chef Cary Neff is a master at creating intense and vivid flavors and exploring gutsy Thai, Mediterranean, and Southwestern cuisine. Throughout his career, he has earned national accolades for multimillion-dollar establishments in Arizona, such as the Scottsdale Princess Resort, the Citadel, the historic Wrigley Mansion Club, the Wigwam Resort, LaCosta, and Miraval Resort and Spa, where he was executive chef for eight years.

Cary has established Conscious Cuisine® as one of the nation's leading spa cuisines. Conscious Cuisine® has been featured in major magazines including *Bon Appetit, Gourmet, Food & Wine, New York Times Magazine,* and *Metropolitan Home,* as well as on *The Oprah Winfrey Show* and *Today.* Chef Neff is currently an active member of the International Association of Culinary Professionals, Chefs Collaborative, and the American Culinary Federation's Apprentice Program.

Jamie Oliver

Jamie Oliver started cooking at his parents' pub at the age of eight and has since worked with some of the world's top chefs, including Antonio Carluccio and Gennaro Contaldo at the Neal Street Restaurant and Rose Gray and Ruth Rogers at the River Cafe. Jamie's five cookbooks have all been international best-sellers, selling over 11 million copies worldwide. His television shows are broadcast in 46 countries. He is co-founder of Fifteen restaurant and involved with the charity Fifteen Foundation, which allows disadvantaged youngsters to become chefs. Currently, Jamie is working on a nationwide campaign to improve school dinners in the U.K.

Apple Pie From *Jamie's Dinners: The Essential Family Cookbook* by Jamie Oliver, © Hyperion 2004.

Charlie Palmer

Charlie Palmer has long been a creative and trendsetting force in American restaurants. Highly respected by his peers, he has been a mentor to the many young chefs in his establishments across the country.

Charlie's upbringing on a farm in upstate New York and his education in various kitchens in France and at the Culinary Institute of America provided him with the basis to form a style and ultimately strike out on his own. At age 28, he opened his first restaurant on Manhattan's Upper Eastside, Aureole. There he continued to hone his craft and create his own signature, "progressive American" style.

Today, Charlie's creativity is still sparked by collaborating with his teams of chefs, cooks, management, and service staff in each of his locations. The chef is also the author of three cookbooks, *Great American Food, Charlie Palmer's Casual Cooking,* and *The Art of Aureole.*

Jacques Pépin

Jacques Pépin is the author of a best-selling memoir, *The Apprentice*, and 21 cookbooks, including the award-winning *Jacques Pépin Celebrates*, *Julia & Jacques: Cooking at Home* (with Julia Child), and most recently *Jacques Pépin: Fast Food My Way.* He has starred in 11 PBS series in the past 20 years.

Before coming to the United States in 1959, Jacques served as the personal chef to three French heads of state, including Charles De Gaulle. A contributing editor to *Food & Wine*, he is the dean of special programs at the French Culinary Institute in New York City and teaches at Boston University. He has won many awards including numerous James Beard Awards, IACP Cookbook Awards, and France's highest honors, the Chevalier des Arts et Lettres and the Legion d'Honneur. He lives with his wife, Gloria, in Madison, Connecticut.

Steven Raichlen

Steven Raichlen is a multi-award-winning author, journalist, cooking teacher, and TV host. His best-selling books and *Barbecue University* TV show on PBS have virtually reinvented American barbecue. His 26 books include *The Barbecue Bible*, *How to Grill*, *BBQ USA*, *Beer Can Chicken*, *Sauces, Rubs, and Marinades*, and *Raichlen's Indoor Grilling* (all published by Workman).

In 2000, Steven founded Barbecue University, a unique cooking school headquartered at The Greenbrier resort in White Sulfur Springs, West Virginia. He is also creator of the Steven Raichlen "Best of Barbecue" line of grilling tools, fuels, flavorings, and accessories.

In 1975, Steven received a Thomas J. Watson Foundation Fellowship to study medieval cooking in Europe, as well as a Fulbright Scholarship to study comparative literature. He holds a degree in French literature from Reed College and trained at the Cordon Bleu and La Varenne cooking schools in Paris. Steven lives with his wife, Barbara, in Coconut Grove, Florida.

Aaron Sanchez

As a former co-host of Food Network's "Melting Pot," Aaron introduced a national audience to his technique and creativity with contemporary interpretations of classic Latin cuisine. His audience can sample this fare at his restaurant, Paladar, located in New York City, as well as at Mixx Restaurant in the Borgata Hotel and Spa in Atlantic City. Aaron has vivid childhood memories of helping his mother, Zarela, prepare traditional Mexican foods for her catering business in El Paso Texas. By the time Aaron was 11, the family had moved to New York City, and Zarela launched Café Marimba, giving Aaron his first taste of professional cooking life.

Today, Aaron is a restaurateur, television personality, consultant, spokesperson, and author. His first book, *La Comida del Barrio,* was published in 2003. Aaron makes international appearances conducting cooking classes where he shares his passion for Latin cuisine with thousands of admirers throughout the year.

Sal J. Scognamillo

Salvatore (Sal) Scognamillo is a co-owner and third-generation executive chef of the world-renowned Patsy's restaurant, still at its one and only location, 236 West 56th Street in New York City. Trained by his father, Joe, and his grandfather, Pasquale "Patsy" before him, Sal Scognamillo has maintained the same level of comfort and quality that made Patsy's famous more than 60 years ago. In 1985, upon his father's retirement from the kitchen, Sal assumed the position of executive chef.

Since taking over the kitchen at Patsy's, Sal has continued to prepare the original Neapolitan recipes that his grandfather cooked before him. Over the past 20 years, he has overseen the expansion of Patsy's empire to include jar sauces, prepared foods, oils and vinegars, and the best-selling *Patsy's Cookbook: Classic Italian Recipes from a New York City Landmark Restaurant.* Patsy's was, and remains, a family restaurant. Sal co-owns the restaurant with his father, Joe, and cousin, Frank DiCola.

Scotto Family

Fresco by Scotto Restaurant opened in November 1993. It's well-known as the power broker's lunch and star-filled entertainment industry diner and is often referred to as the "NBC Commissary." The restaurant is owned and operated by the Scotto family—Marion, Rosanna, Elaina, and Anthony Jr.

Fresco by Scotto has received outstanding reviews in *New York Magazine, Gourmet Magazine, The New York Times,* and 3 Stars in *Crain's New York Business.* The Scotto family members have appeared in cooking segments on NBC's *Today, The Rosie O'Donnell Show,* and *Extra.*

B. Smith

B. Smith, lifestyle expert, TV personality, restaurateur, author, and former model, has served for the last eight years as host of *B. Smith with Style,* the only nationally syndicated half-hour lifestyle television series hosted by an African American. She is owner of three successful B. Smith restaurants located in New York, Washington, D. C., and Sag Harbor, New York. The B. Smith Restaurant Group was formed in 1998 and is in the process of expanding its holdings.

A seasoned culinary and lifestyle expert, B. Smith was recognized by *Elle Décor* magazine as one of America's 10 most outstanding nonprofessional chefs. She is also the first African-American woman elected to the Board of Trustees of the Culinary Institute of America. B. has brought her hot tips and effervescent personality to television with guest appearances on *The Oprah Winfrey Show,* NBC's *Today,* and ABC's *Good Morning America.*

Suzanne Somers

Suzanne Somers is the author of 13 books, including the *New York Times* best-sellers *Keeping Secrets; Eat Great, Lose Weight; Get Skinny on Fabulous Food; Eat, Cheat, and Melt the Fat Away; Fast and Easy;* and *The Sexy Years.* Her books currently have more than 10 million copies in print. In a multifaceted career that has spanned nearly three decades, she has achieved extraordinary success as an actress, singer, comedienne, author, entrepreneur, and lecturer. She was the star of the hit televisions programs *Three's Company, She's the Sheriff,* and *Step by Step.* Today, 5 million Somersizers keep to Suzanne's recommended regimen of exercise and smart eating to stay fit and feel fabulous.

215

Ivy Stark

As corporate chef of Rosa Mexicano, Ivy Stark oversees day-to-day operations and collaborates with culinary director Roberto Santibañez on the upscale, authentic Mexican cuisine for which the restaurants are known and loved. Born in Colorado, Stark's passion for Latin cuisine has led her to work at some of the country's top restaurants.

She began her culinary career at the Institute for Culinary Education in New York before moving to Los Angeles to apprentice with celebrity chefs Mary Sue Milliken and Susan Feniger at Border Grill. Ivy would later work with the pair as opening chef at their pan-Latin restaurant, Ciudad. Returning to New York City, Ivy served as executive chef at Dos Caminos, Zocalo, Match Uptown, and executive sous chef at Cena. She has earned a certificate from the American Sommelier Association and graduated from UCLA with a B.A. in history.

Alice Waters

Alice Waters is the owner of Chez Panisse restaurant in Berkeley, California. Over the last three decades, Chez Panisse has cultivated a network of local farmers who share the restaurant's commitment to sustainable agriculture. In 2001, Chez Panisse was named best restaurant in the United States by *Gourmet* magazine. Alice initiated the Edible Schoolyard project in 1995, which incorporates her ideas about food and culture into the public school curriculum. She has published eight books, the most recent of which is *Chez Panisse Fruit* (HarperCollins, 2002).

Liz Weiss

A Registered Dietitian, Liz Weiss is co-author of *The Moms' Guide to Meal Makeovers: Improving the Way Your Family Eats, One Meal at a Time* (Broadway Books, 2004). With co-author Janice Bissex, she founded the Meal Makeover Moms Club at **www.mealmakeovermoms.com,** creating an online community for parents. Liz is a contributing editor for *Health* magazine and writes a monthly column for *Nick Jr. Family Magazine.* She is a former producer and correspondent for CNN's *On The Menu* and the PBS series *HealthWeek.* Liz received her undergraduate degree in nutrition from the University of Rhode Island, her master's in nutrition communications from Boston University, and completed the Professional Chef's Program at the Cambridge School of Culinary Arts. She lives in Massachusetts with her husband and two young sons, Josh and Simon.

>Index

>Celebrity Chefs and Guests

METRIC INFORMATION

The charts on this page provide a guide for converting measurements from the U.S. customary system, which is used throughout this book, to the metric system.

Product Differences

Most of the ingredients called for in the recipes in this book are available in most countries. However, some are known by different names. Here are some common American ingredients and their possible counterparts:

> All-purpose flour is enriched, bleached or unbleached white household flour. When self-rising flour is used in place of all-purpose flour in a recipe that calls for leavening, omit the leavening agent (baking soda or baking powder) and salt.
> Baking soda is bicarbonate of soda.
> Cornstarch is cornflour.
> Golden raisins are sultanas.
> Green, red, or yellow sweet peppers are capsicums or bell peppers.
> Light-colored corn syrup is golden syrup.
> Powdered sugar is icing sugar.
> Sugar (white) is granulated, fine granulated, or castor sugar.
> Vanilla or vanilla extract is vanilla essence.

Volume & Weight

The United States traditionally uses cup measures for liquid and solid ingredients. The chart below shows the approximate imperial and metric equivalents. If you are accustomed to weighing solid ingredients, the following approximate equivalents will be helpful.

> 1 cup butter, castor sugar, or rice = 8 ounces = ½ pound = 250 grams
> 1 cup flour = 4 ounces = ¼ pound = 125 grams
> 1 cup icing sugar = 5 ounces = 150 grams

Canadian and U.S. volume for a cup measure is 8 fluid ounces (237 ml), but the standard metric equivalent is 250 ml.

1 British imperial cup is 10 fluid ounces.

In Australia, 1 tablespoon equals 20 ml, and there are 4 teaspoons in the Australian tablespoon.

Spoon measures are used for smaller amounts of ingredients. Although the size of the tablespoon varies slightly in different countries, for practical purposes and for recipes in this book, a straight substitution is all that's necessary. Measurements made using cups or spoons always should be level unless stated otherwise.

Common Weight Range Replacements

Imperial / U.S.	Metric
½ ounce	15 g
1 ounce	25 g or 30 g
4 ounces (¼ pound)	115 g or 125 g
8 ounces (½ pound)	225 g or 250 g
16 ounces (1 pound)	450 g or 500 g
1¼ pounds	625 g
1½ pounds	750 g
2 pounds or 2¼ pounds	1,000 g or 1 Kg

Oven Temperature Equivalents

Fahrenheit Setting	Celsius Setting*	Gas Setting
300°F	150°C	Gas Mark 2 (very low)
325°F	160°C	Gas Mark 3 (low)
350°F	180°C	Gas Mark 4 (moderate)
375°F	190°C	Gas Mark 5 (moderate)
400°F	200°C	Gas Mark 6 (hot)
425°F	220°C	Gas Mark 7 (hot)
450°F	230°C	Gas Mark 8 (very hot)
475°F	240°C	Gas Mark 9 (very hot)
500°F	260°C	Gas Mark 10 (extremely hot)
Broil	Broil	Grill

*Electric and gas ovens may be calibrated using celsius. However, for an electric oven, increase celsius setting 10 to 20 degrees when cooking above 160°C. For convection or forced air ovens (gas or electric), lower the temperature setting 25°F/10°C when cooking at all heat levels.

Baking Pan Sizes

Imperial / U.S.	Metric
9×1½-inch round cake pan	22- or 23×4-cm (1.5 L)
9×1½-inch pie plate	22- or 23×4-cm (1 L)
8×8×2-inch square cake pan	20×5-cm (2 L)
9×9×2-inch square cake pan	22- or 23×4.5-cm (2.5 L)
11×7×1½-inch baking pan	28×17×4-cm (2 L)
2-quart rectangular baking pan	30×19×4.5-cm (3 L)
13×9×2-inch baking pan	34×22×4.5-cm (3.5 L)
15×10×1-inch jelly roll pan	40×25×2-cm
9×5×3-inch loaf pan	23×13×8-cm (2 L)
2-quart casserole	2 L

U.S. / Standard Metric Equivalents

⅛ teaspoon = 0.5 ml
¼ teaspoon = 1 ml
½ teaspoon = 2 ml
1 teaspoon = 5 ml
1 tablespoon = 15 ml
2 tablespoons = 25 ml
¼ cup = 2 fluid ounces = 50 ml
⅓ cup = 3 fluid ounces = 75 ml
½ cup = 4 fluid ounces = 125 ml
⅔ cup = 5 fluid ounces = 150 ml
¾ cup = 6 fluid ounces = 175 ml
1 cup = 8 fluid ounces = 250 ml
2 cups = 1 pint = 500 ml
1 quart = 1 litre

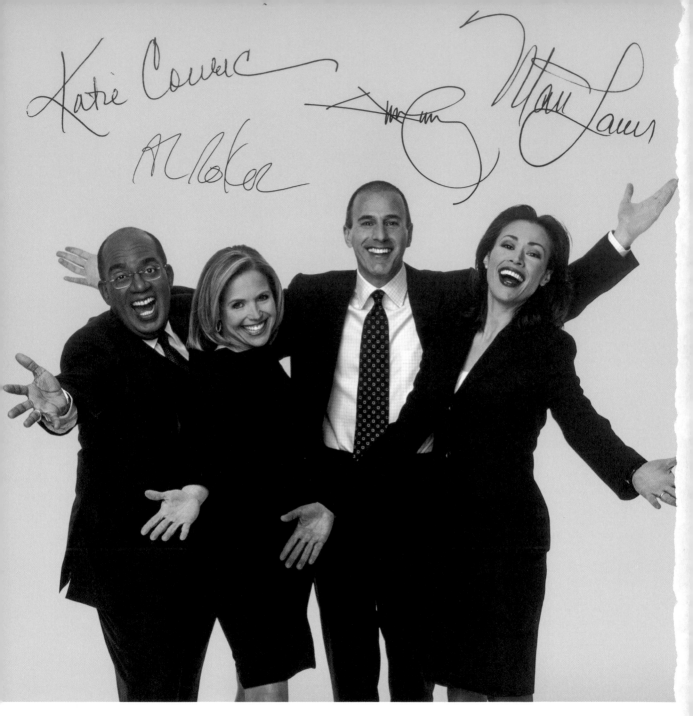

from our family to yours
bon appétit!